CONFESSIONS OF A HAPPY CHRISTIAN

Confessions Of A Happy Christian

by

ZIG ZIGLAR

Foreword by W. A. CRISWELL

PELICAN PUBLISHING COMPANY
Gretna 2004

Copyright © 1978
By Zig Ziglar
All rights reserved

First printing, May 1978
Second printing, November 1979
Third printing, December 1980
Fourth printing, first trade paperback edition,
    August 1982
Fifth printing, May 1985
Sixth printing, July 1993
First Korean edition, September 1998
Seventh printing, April 2004

Library of Congress Cataloging in Publication Data

Ziglar, Zig.
  Confessions of a happy Christian.

  1. Christian life—Baptist authors. 2.
Ziglar, Zig. I. Title.
BV4501.2.Z54   248'.48'61   78-6729
ISBN 0-88289-400-5

Manufactured in the United States of America

Published by Pelican Publishing Company, Inc.
1000 Burmaster Street, Gretna, Louisiana 70053

Designed by Barney McKee

TO

My mother and mother-in-law. Two great ladies whose faith in this life gained for them a comfortable and everlasting seat in the audience of the Lord.

Contents

Foreword

Would you like to sit down and have a heart-to-heart talk with one of the most delightful businessmen in America? Then read this book, entitled *Confessions of A Happy Christian*, by Zig Ziglar. Would you like to spend an evening in one of the most delightful pursuits that you could ever follow? Then read this book by one of God's brightest servants, Zig Ziglar. Would you like to know how to live an abundant life full of real joy and supernal happiness? Then follow these recipes that have been offered to us by Zig Ziglar.

Any minister in the world would love my assignment of having the opportunity to write an introduction to *Confessions of A Happy Christian*. These chapters are not speculative and theoretical; they arise out of the actual day-to-day confrontation with life as Zig Ziglar has experienced it down the road of this earthly pilgrimage. His Christian commitment turns ten thousand facets of the ever-changing spectrum of existence into an endless series of victories and triumphs. Because he loves Jesus he is never discouraged, for he has found the key to triumphant living. He never senses failure in any providence or in any sorrow. God is with him, and through him we sense the same presence of the Spirit of the Lord in our own souls.

Zig Ziglar lives what he writes. His faith and his religion are not hollow sentences and syllables, but they are realities and revelations upon which he is building an incomparably glorious life. Listening to Zig, we are persuaded that we can live the same kind of life and follow the same kind of a road to ultimate victory. Fortunate is the person who opens this book and reads these heavenly chapters written by a gloriously happy Christian.

First Baptist Church   W. A. CRISWELL
Dallas, Texas

Thank You

Mother, for loving me so much you always acted in my best interests by taking me into God's house whether I wanted to go or not. Mrs. Ab for raising Jean in such a special, loving way under God's direction so that she became an ideal help-mate for me.

Thank you Tom for being "an harassment committee of one," as God used you to prod me into Bible study so I could answer some of your never-ending questions. And thank you Suzan, Cindy, and Julie for your love, understanding, and encouragement all of your lives, but especially during those first few months after I made my commitment to serve Jesus Christ. What a thrill it has been to me to watch your own faith grow!

Thank you preachers, teachers, and fellow Christians. Your sharing of your love and faith has been meaningful and encouraging beyond words during these few short years I have walked with the Lord. A special thank you to Dr. and Mrs. W. A. Criswell, my pastor and my teacher, who regularly explore my needs and collaborate to teach an entire lesson and preach a full sermon just for me (at least that's the way it seems!).

Thank you, staff members, for carrying an extra load for me so that I could be free to spend the countless hours necessary to complete the manuscript. A double thank-you, Laurie Magers. Not only have you functioned with increasing effectiveness as my executive assistant while typing, retyping, and then typing this manuscript again, again, and yet again, but your expressions of appreciation regarding the meaningfulness of the message in your own personal life have been most beneficial.

Thank you Nancy and Milburn Calhoun—to Milburn for your vote of confidence in making this book your largest single printing; to Nancy for your praise and enthusiasm as you read the first rough draft of the manuscript. This gave me a tremendous boost and encouraged me to multiply my efforts and get the completed manuscript published and in the hands of those who thirst after the Good News of Jesus Christ.

Most importantly—thank you "Sugar Baby," for being lovingly and exclusively mine. My love for you grows daily, and my gratitiude for your help and insight in helping me keep my eyes on the Savior knows no bounds. Your specific thoughts and suggestions on *Confessions* will surely be meaningful to many.

Finally, to the many, many Christian brothers and sisters who have shared their faith, spiritual insights, and "goodies," your help has been tremendous, needed, and deeply appreciated. God bless you all, have a good forever, and I truly will SEE YOU AT THE TOP—up there!

Introduction

Confessions started out in my mind as a booklet about ten pages long, but as you can see, it grew. Originally, I planned to share a few simple thoughts about my own life and what it meant to turn that life over to Jesus. However, as I started praying, writing, and thinking, it became more and more obvious that I could never communicate the message God had laid on my heart in just a few pages.

Essentially, there are three major messages I hope to share with you. Number one is obviously my love for and joy in my salvation through the shed blood of Jesus Christ. Number two, I want to share the tremendous excitement and innumerable benefits that are yours *now* if you turn your life over to Jesus Christ. Number three, I would like to put to bed the absurd notion that Christians are supposed to have long faces and short pocketbooks.

This book is really more in praise of our Lord than anything else. Hopefully, God will use this message to help ease your journey along the way of life. Many of the phrases, examples, and illustrations have come from friends, sermons, pamphlets, and everyday life. I make no pretense or claim to be a Bible scholar or even a good Bible student, but I do feel that God wants me to share His love through this book. It is written entirely for His glory. I have felt His Presence as I have written, and on many occasions, as I wrote of the total love of Jesus, my eyes filled and I had to stop writing. On other occasions I would get so excited and happy I would be hard put not to laugh or shout. The only thing that was constant and consistent as I wrote was my feeling of God's presence and love.

As you read my confessions, you will note that I make a lot of references to my family and to my church, which happens to be Southern Baptist. It is my prayer that *no one* who reads this would think for one minute that I am implying that you have to be a Baptist to be saved or born again. It is my prayer that *everyone* who reads *Confessions of A Happy Christian* will get the message that you must know Jesus—and no one else—to be saved.

Today I worship at Prestonwood Baptist Church, because they preach and teach that *all* of the Bible—and *only* the Bible—is the inspired Word of God. I urge you to go to a church, any church, that teaches the same thing. The church does not save you; Jesus Christ saves you, and that faith comes by hearing the Word. So, you *need* to go to a church where they teach what God has to say. Unfortunately, in many of the churches today, you hear everything preached *but* God's Word. As a matter of fact, a preacher has been defined as a mild-mannered man speaking a mild-mannered message to a mild-mannered congregation about how to be more mild mannered—and that simply is not what church or Jesus Christ is all about. You can read the papers, listen to the radio, and watch television all week and you can hear what man says about man's problems. On Sunday, you need to be in God's house hearing what God has to say about solving man's problems.

In *Confessions,* I am going to confess from "hello" to "goodbye" the *good news* the Bible is stocked with. Instead of, as the song says, "where seldom is heard, a discouraging word," you are not going to hear *any* discouraging words. You are going to hear words of hope, power, love, strength, reward, victory, excitement, plenty, comfort, and encouragement. The reason is simple: God tells us in Proverbs 18:20-21: "With the fruit of a man's mouth his stomach will be satisfied; He will be satisfied with the product of his lips. Death and life are in the power of the tongue, And those who love it will eat its fruit." Now think about what God said and you will get excited about and understand why I'm going to confess the good things about my

Lord. Bookstores, newsstands, television, radio, and, tragically, too many pulpits confess all the things that are negative and wrong. Say "confession" in the church you attend and to most of the people you know, and the vast majority will think you are talking about confessing sins, sickness, weakness, want, and failure. *This* is not *that* kind of confession. I'm going to confess the *good* things God gives us.

Any shade-tree psychologist will tell you exactly what God tells you in Job 3:2-5: "That which I have feared greatly has come upon me." Or, as ye sow, so also shall ye reap. Your doctor will tell you that if you plant negative thoughts, you can *literally* induce sickness and even premature death. Last year while I was in Australia with my wife and son, we were told on good authority that in the "outback" some tribes of Australian aborigines believe that if a witchdoctor points a bone at them (any kind of bone) they will die. Documented cases of this practice state that in a matter of hours the victims are not feeling well and in a matter of days they are *dead.* Now before you shake your head and mutter, "poor, ignorant, superstitious natives," let me ask you a question. Are you living a happy, victorious life? When people see you do they see the *real* Jesus in you, or do they see a downcast, non-existent, defeated pseudo-Jesus? If it's the latter, then hold onto your hat and keep reading because I have some good news for you! It's the *Confessions of A Happy Christian*—ME!

In *Confessions,* starting immediately, I'm going to share with you why you should not—must not—confess the negativisms of life. I might add that the next few sentences are critical to one of the primary objectives of this book, namely, to help you to live a joyful, Jesus-controlled, victorious life—NOW.

Since Satan is a created being and was beaten in combat by our Lord, we know he is no match for Jesus Christ. He cannot read our minds, intercept our thoughts, or tell the future. However, Satan is resourceful, deceitful, and imaginative, knows the Bible, and is committed to your destruction. The best possible way to aid Satan in your destruction is to stay away from your Bible and constantly tell him your troubles and weaknesses. When you confess your troubles to anyone who will listen, you are simply revealing the weak link in your armor to Satan. You let him know where you are weak and vulnerable. Then Satan goes to work with a vengeance. Statements such as, "When it rains, it pours," "If it's not one thing, it's another," or "Troubles come in bunches," invite Satan's personal attention. Announce that you "didn't sleep a wink all night"; that you "don't feel very well"; "have a splitting headache"; are "having trouble making ends meet"; "had a big quarrel with your neighbor"; tell the neighbor or the people at work the details of your marital problems; or a thousand and one other problems and you are giving Satan an engraved invitation to come into your life and compound your problems. It would be oversimplifying the problem to say that Satan always comes in through an open mouth, but I am right when I tell you that when you open your mouth and confess your problems you give Satan all the opening he needs.

IMPORTANT—VERY IMPORTANT

I am not talking about going to a Christian brother or sister or a counselor who is skilled in solving the type problem you have (doctor, lawyer, minister, etc.). You go to these people and confess for the sole purpose of solving the problem. That's different, especially if you meet in Jesus's name and in His presence, seeking divine guidance and thanking Him for solving the problem. That's not only permissible—it's positive. I'm obviously not talking about your going to God in prayer and telling Him about your problem. As a matter of fact, that's the first step to take. When you talk to Jesus, there is no possibility that Satan will intercept the message and exert a power greater than our Lord's.

One request please: Since I can cover only one subject or thought at a time, I hope you will read the entire book and keep all of it in perspective. It is written under conviction, in love, over a period of sixteen months, with the prayer and hope that it will be helpful in leading you toward a more meaningful and loving relationship with Jesus Christ as Lord and Savior.

CONFESSIONS OF A HAPPY CHRISTIAN

CHAPTER ONE

A Declaration of Dependence

On July 4, 1776, thirteen isolated colonies declared their *independence* from Great Britain, an event that shook the world and changed the course of history. On July 4, 1972, I declared my complete *dependence* on Jesus Christ, an event which completely changed my own personal, family, and business life.

From that moment on, God looked past my faults and saw my needs. He immediately showed me that He could and would replace everything that was missing in my life, but that nothing could replace Him in my life.

One thing I stress, Even though I claim July 4 as my "born again" day, I'm not certain that it actually happened that day. I am certain it happened during that weekend. For me, there was no clanging of bells or flashing of lights. There was a warm, solid feeling of complete confidence that God saw my heart, heard my confession of sin, and welcomed me into His Kingdom when I acknowledged Jesus Christ as Lord *and* Savior *and* master of my life.

It's important that you understand this because many people, maybe including you, never have that earth-shattering moment of ecstacy. If you don't or didn't, don't be concerned. You are not saved by a feeling, but by trusting God and accepting Jesus Christ as your Savior.

As the earth revolves around the sun, so should our lives also revolve around the Son.

When asked what he knew about God, George Beverly Shea replied, "Not much, but what I do know has changed by life!"

When you turn to God you discover He has been facing you all the time.

You can no more do God's work without God than you could have sunshine without the sun.

Repentance: Being sorry for what you've done and sorry enough to do something about it.

One reason I love the Lord so much is explained in Luke 7:47: "But to whom little is forgiven, the same loveth little." In my case, much was forgiven, so I love much.

CHAPTER TWO

Positive Christianity

I was coming into Dallas on a plane—which is generally the way I fly—and noticed that the fellow next to me had his wedding band on the index finger of his right hand. I couldn't resist the temptation to comment, so I said, "Friend, I can't help but notice that you've got your wedding band on the wrong finger."

He smiled and replied, "Yeah, I married the wrong woman."

I do not know whether he married the wrong woman or not, but I do know that many Christians and *all* non-Christians have the wrong idea about what it means to know Jesus Christ personally.

THE "NEGATIVE" CHRISTIAN

Many times I hear people talk about someone being a "negative" Christian. I challenge the terminology. I'm convinced that you can either be negative or you can be a Christian, but you can no more be negative and Christian than you can be Christian and Communist. The two are incompatible. Christians, if I understand it correctly, have the complete assurance that if we ask God, He not only will forgive us of our past sins, He will forget them as well. That takes care of the past. Jesus Christ said, "I am come that they might have life, and that they might have it more abundantly." That obviously takes care of the present. Psalm 23, as well as John 3:16, assures us that as believers we will dwell in the house of the Lord forever. That certainly takes care of the future. Since a Christian has his past forgiven, his present secured, and his future irrevocably guaranteed, please tell me why or *how* a Christian should or could be negative? I'm not saying a Christian never has a "down" moment or a negative thought. That's unrealistic. I'm talking about his basic nature.

Now in case you think this reasoning is either too simplistic or too optimistic, I urge you to read your Bible carefully. I challenge you to show me *one* discouraging incident or thought *after* the resurrection. Even Thomas became an unshakable believer when he thrust his hand into the spear-pierced side of our Lord. Christ used that occasion—as He does *all* occasions for His—to teach a powerful lesson in faith. Since we worship a resurrected Lord, a living Savior, this provides the believer with what we need to live a victorious life.

I often hear the phrase "Sunday Christians," but the more I think about it, the more I am convinced these people do not exist. It is true that there are some who go to church on Sunday, dutifully carrying their Bibles, paying their stipend to the church, adjusting their halos, and rubbing souls with the saints while planning to go back to the business community on Monday and prove how adept they are at manipulating people for their own personal gains. But I repeat, there is no such thing as a "Sunday Christian"; there are people who go to church on Sunday who say they are Christians. When Christ takes over a life, it's a total takeover—not one day a week, or even two or three; it is a complete takeover, twenty-four hours of every day. This is not to say that Christians will live perfect, sinless lives, because they will not. But it does mean that when a Christian knowingly sins, God puts a burden on him which he simply cannot bear until he confesses and makes it right.

I often challenge my fellow Christians with this thought: Suppose a person who did not know Jesus were to follow you for a week, and then follow one of Satan's disciples for a week. Based on what he saw in you as far as love, joy, happiness, and peace of mind, would that person follow Satan or would he follow our Lord? Let's face it, many non-Christians are aware of what you do and will partially make their decisions on what they see in you. What a responsibility and opportunity.

MAMA, WHAT IN THE WORLD IS THAT?

I am of the opinion that Christians should be like the story of the mama skunk and the baby skunks going by the paper mill. (If you've ever been close to a paper mill, you'll get the drift of this right away.) One of the baby skunks, almost overcome by the odor, sniffed the air and said, "Mama, what in the world is that?" Mama skunk sniffed and answered, "I don't know, but we've sure got to get some of it!" I believe, as Christians, we need to live an exuberant, joyful life so that when anyone sees us they will automatically say, "I don't know what that person has, but whatever it is, I've got to get some of it!"

I love what John Wright, a successful young real estate executive from Indianapolis, says. When people ask him what he eventually wants to be, he smiles and says, "Contagious." John truly wants the love and power of Jesus to be so dominant and beautiful that he will become so contagious people will "catch" Jesus from him. That's exciting. John also emphasizes that, "If you pray you don't need to worry—and if you don't pray, it does you no good to worry." Don't misunderstand. I'm not suggesting that you go around with a forced smile on your face all the time (though I'm convinced that an insincere smile is better than a sincere frown). Nor am I suggesting that everything is always 100 percent good for Christians, because it isn't. However, if we really do believe that God selects the best for us when we give Him the choice, that everything crosses His desk before it happens, and as believers we are to thank Him for *everything* that happens, then it seems to me that God might question our sincerity when we demonstrate our thanks to Him with a long, sad face. Since we are our brother's keeper, and since the first and last thing our Lord commanded us to do was to witness for Him, then a pleasant, cheerful countenance is extremely important.

Question: As an individual, don't you enjoy being around the cheerful optimist more than being around the kind of person who could brighten up a whole room—just by leaving it?

THE JOY OF BEING A CHRISTIAN

Under no circumstances would I ever want anyone to think I take my faith in my Lord lightly or in anything approaching a frivolous way. Actually, I shed far more tears nowadays than I did before I turned my life over to Jesus Christ, but they are usually tears of joy and victory and not of bitterness or defeat. As I read my Scriptures and make an effort to live a Christian life, I am convinced that joy, laughter, and humor are integral parts of everyday life. Throughout the Scriptures we read references to joy. As a matter of fact, when an abundant life is mentioned or implied, joy is a frequent companion. In the story of the talents, when the Lord spoke to the two men who multiplied their talents, He concluded the analogy by saying, "Enter ye into the *joy* of the Lord." Solomon said, "A merry heart hath a continual feast." I believe the old approach to serving our Lord has probably done as much damage as it has done good. If a nonbeliever perceives a Christian as a harsh, stern-faced, never-smiling, joyless individual, the nonbeliever, in most cases, would want no part of that kind of Christianity.

One of Satan's most effective tools has been his success in selling the idea that, to really have fun, you've got to run with Satan's crowd. As one who has walked both sides of the street, I can tell you that the average member of Satan's crowd *appears* to be having more fun than the average Christian. If the individual who is committed neither to Christ nor to Satan views the long-faced Christian group or the typical fun-seeking worldly crowd, he is probably going to confuse temporary pleasure with happiness and be tempted to cast his lot with Satan. Wouldn't it be tragic if someone saw the misery on the face or in the actions of a Christian and said, "If that's Christianity, deliver me!" I'm convinced that the Lord expects us to experience and then to demonstrate His joy, His excitement, His enthusiasm, and zest for living. That way, when people see us they can say, "That's what I want to be," or, "That's the way I want to be." We can do our best by being happy—and letting our faces know it. (Smile, Brother, smile—the practice will be good for you.)

As I write I'm going to repeatedly make reference to the *now* benefits of serving Jesus Christ. I'm going to constantly parade you by the heavenly smorgasbord that is available to you and me. The beautiful thing about this smorgasbord is the fact that you can constantly eat from it and never grow fat, sassy, or complacent. As a matter of fact, the more you eat from it the more thoughtful, caring, loving, kind, and considerate you will become. That's natural, because God Himself set the table and every good and perfect gift comes from above. There are lots of goodies on the menu as you shall see, but surely your appetite and curiosity are sufficiently whetted to urge you down the line to look at some of the entrees.

ONE OF THE FIRST ENTREES IS LOVE

Had you asked me if I really loved my wife prior to knowing Jesus Christ, I emphatically would have assured you I did, because to the best of my ability I did love my wife. But once Christ entered the picture and I understood that each of us lives forever, then I entered into a new and far greater dimension of love. I loved her before in my own way; I love her today in the way that our Lord would have me love her. The relationship is so much more beautiful, so much more complete, so much more exciting.

Had you asked about my love for my children, I would have assured you—and I'm completely confident they would have, too—that my love for them was beyond calculation. It was beyond *my* calculation, but Jesus Christ, Creator of the universe, added a dimension of love that literally has no limits. When you look at your own and *know* they are God's own children with souls that will live forever, your love takes on a new dimension. You now love them through Christ and as He would have you to love them. The difference is enormous.

Had you asked about my love for my fellow man, I would have assured you that, indeed, I did love my fellow man. I would have explained that my entire work life was wrapped up in helping my fellow man reach his objectives. Even then I knew

I could more effectively help my fellow man by loving him. In retrospect I now realize the love I felt was pale by comparison to the love I now feel. I'm convinced that God has taken this new dimension of love and blessed it in a multitude of ways.

CHRISTIANITY—THE "GIVE UP" RELIGION

Tragically, there are literally millions of people who know the name of Jesus Christ, but who know nothing of the love and saving grace of Christ as Lord and Savior. Many people think of Christ as the Savior who takes instead of the Savior who gave His life to give us our lives. They believe, as I did, that if they turn their lives over to Christ they will have to give up a variety of things. There are literally millions of people who know they should and eventually plan to turn their lives over to the Lord. In the meantime, they still have some "habits" that aren't "really that bad" which they do not want to give up. In some cases, they rationalize, "I'll do it later." Sometimes they justify their actions with a self-induced doubt about whether or not there really is an eternity. They feel that since they are enjoying what they are doing they can see no real reason to give up a sure fun thing here on planet earth for a maybe fun thing in eternity. Additionally, they practice the golden rule, and if they are wrong they aren't hurting anybody but themselves. Old Satan has worked overtime selling this concept. With this in mind, I dedicate this book to the beauties and advantages of serving our Lord and Savior Jesus Christ totally and completely, from this moment on.

Here is something I've said a thousand times since my venture into the saving grace of Jesus Christ on that magnificent July day in 1972, when I irrevocably committed my life to Him. If there were no eternity, if when they lowered me into the grave it was all over, if I made any changes in my lifestyle, it would be to serve Christ even more enthusiastically. The things I have gained thus far from serving Christ are beyond measure. The peace, joy and excitement, and the relationship with my wife and my fellow man now compared to the way things were before I came to know Christ as a living Savior cannot be described.

The extra power the Lord has given me as I live through Him, the effectiveness in my profession, and the love of my fellow human beings all add up to a substantial number of reasons for serving the Lord *now*. Eternity is my bonus. Admittedly, it's a colossal bonus. But, the *now* benefits of serving Christ are also immense.

I CONFESS: I DID GIVE UP SOME THINGS

I will confess there are some things I have given up since I accepted Christ. I gave up staying awake at night, because I realized the Lord is going to be up anyway. I've given up worrying about tomorrow because I know He is already there. I've given up my concern about financial obligations because I realize that the Lord is just as concerned with my needs—even before I have them—as I am. Since He has the resources of the universe to handle the situation, I don't believe it's necessary for me to add my less-than-two-cents to the solution. Don't misunderstand. As I've repeatedly said, the Lord has kept me busier than ever, but I've always been busy. Faith added effectiveness to my busyness and success to my business.

Please—oh, double please—don't misread the above paragraph. All too often I encounter Christian brothers and sisters who say they are just "in the Word" and "trusting the Lord" for all their needs. Oftentimes they will even criticize other less pious brothers in the faith because they are actually busy working and not praying and studying all the time. These people often are confused themselves and hence confuse a lot of others. I don't question their sincerity but it's kind of like the bull standing on the railroad track facing an oncoming train—you admire his courage but you question his judgment. The Lord I worship is so practical that He tells us to pray for our daily bread *before* we ask for forgiveness for our sins. That's practical, and I believe He expects us to be practical and not become so heavenly minded we're no earthly good. I love the story of the two little boys on their way to school. One of them suddenly looked at his watch and exclaimed, "We're going to be late!

We'd better stop and pray." The other was far more practical, so he said, "No, we'd better run—and pray while we run!"

Another favorite is the one about the farmer who bought the weed-riddled, run-down farm and through an enormous amount of hard, back-breaking work turned it into a beautiful and productive farm. One day one of the local brethren stopped by for a visit and after a time observed that the Lord sure had been good to him in giving him such a beautiful and productive farm. To this the farmer, who must have been a practicing, working Christian, said, "Yes, He sure has, but you should have seen this place when the Lord had it by Himself!"

As I write this book, the salesman in me probably will be very evident. I believe the greatest single mistake Christians make is not using sales knowledge and common sense in spreading the word about the benefits of walking through *this* life with Jesus Christ. With the greatest product in existence to sell, many Christians talk about nothing but what will happen if you don't serve the Lord and "do right." They present judgment and hell as a steady diet. That's fear motivation and it works temporarily for some, but I'm convinced that a lost and often discouraged world needs to repeatedly hear about the *love* of Jesus.

BE A SALESMAN FOR JESUS

One of the first things I was taught as a salesman was not to knock the competition. Why advertise for them? If comparisons were made, we were instructed to spend our time pointing out the facts and benefits of *our* product. In the Christian community we spend too much time downgrading those who do not believe exactly as we do. The result is that we often work so hard at becoming "theologically as straight as a gun barrel that we end up as empty as one spiritually." We talk too much about what people ought not to do instead of selling the benefits that go with loving and serving Jesus.

As a salesman, I've sold everything from cookware, soap, and life insurance to books, vitamins, and cassette recordings. I have never sold anything that I was not sold on myself, so I was enthusiastic about *all* the products I sold. Now, if I could—and did—get enthusiastic about these products, doesn't it make sense that I could *really* get enthusiastic about Jesus Christ? Just think—a Lord whom it would be absolutely *impossible* to oversell. Now that's a salesman's dream! You can't overstate or oversell His love, His care, His concern, or His power to fulfill *every* promise He makes.

I can say this with enthusiasm because I'm a satisfied customer who has shopped in the marketplace of Satan and in the eternal love of Jesus Christ. I listened to Satan's subtle, lying promises and gave him far too many of the first forty-five years of my life. Then I listened to the promises of Jesus, and I confess to you that the best thing going on planet earth is Jesus Christ. I never had it so good—never had so much love, peace, joy, happiness, security, and contentment along with better physical, mental, and spiritual health. My career is moving along far better under the leadership of the Eternal Director, and I have made more financial progress in the last seven years than I did the preceding forty-five years. Since I like *all* of those advantages, I would never go back to serving Satan. In short, I'm committed to serving Christ.

DON'T MISUNDERSTAND

I believe—no, I *know*—that Satan and hell exist in a very real sense. I work at avoiding Satan and I will avoid hell. I agree that we must let the nonbelievers know that God is not only a loving God, but that He is a just and judging God. I believe we must let them know that it is an awful thing to feel the wrath of God and that hell is a real place we want to avoid. *But* I also believe that the positive selling of our Savior is far better than negatively selling the horrors of eternal damnation. In short, I believe as does Dallas architect Ralph Brummet that it is far better to feed the sheep than it is to beat the sheep.

As an earthly father, I deeply and dearly love my children. When they were small I used a certain amount of applied psychology, which I attempted to apply with reasonable firmness at the right time and in the right place. Each child knew there were certain things they could not do and boundaries which they could not exceed without retribution. However, for every time I raised my hand for punishment I raised it a thousand times in love. Now if I, an earthly father, used the thousand-to-one ratio, how much more does our Heavenly Father shower His love versus His punishment on His? As we dig into God's promises and select the good things from that Heavenly smorgasbord, God really spells it out for us in Matthew 7:11, when Jesus tells us "that if you then being evil know how to give good gifts unto your children, how much more shall your Father which is in Heaven give good things to them that ask Him?" Not only does He know what to give us, but He has the resources of the universal supermarket from which to select our gifts.

Think about it for a moment; when you compare the wealth of our Heavenly Father to the wealth of man on earth the comparison is ridiculous. For example, Bill Gates is reputedly worth billions of dollars. However, those billions of dollars would not feed the fishes of the sea or the birds of the air for a single day. Our Heavenly Father feeds them forever. And don't forget that as co-heirs with Jesus (Romans 8:17) we *inherit* the universe. Not only does He have the resources, but He tells us in Matthew 6:8, "Be not ye therefore like unto them for your Father knoweth what things you have need of before you ask Him." The Lord, who *has* everything we need, also *knows* our needs *before* we even think about them. And He is anxious to give them to us who are His. I'm convinced He wants us to have some of them *now* while we need them and so we can enjoy them on planet earth.

TALKING ABOUT COMMITMENT

As I was putting the finishing touches to this book, we were busy at our church collecting pledge cards so we could meet our budget. Richard Peacock, our Godly minister to the adults, pointed out that we pledge ourselves to our mates, to making house payments, car payments, and a thousand and one other facets of our daily lives. Most people make these commitments without a great deal of thought and accept them as necessary. However, they come up with a dozen reasons why they won't pledge to give back to God just a tenth of what is already His anyway. The classic or standard reasoning goes something like this (with a mild halo adjustment thrown in): "Well, I do the best I can, but I never know what the future holds and when I make a commitment I live up to it." Amazing, isn't it? Christians who are willing to commit to everything and everybody, but are reluctant and even refuse to commit a few dollars for one year to Jesus Christ. In short, they refuse or fear to sign a pledge card.

THINK ABOUT THIS

EVERYTHING I have (some of this will probably apply to you) or own that has any real value came to me as a result of signing my name. God gave me a beautiful woman fifty-seven years ago for my very own. But I could not claim her until, in the presence of Him, His minister, and witnesses, I signed my name to the marriage vows. Later, God gave me three beautiful daughters and a handsome son, but I could not claim them for my own and take them out of the hospital until I had signed my name. My family, car, life insurance program, and investments all came to me only after I had signed my name to a pledge. *All* of these things bring me a certain amount of comfort, and I'm delighted to have all of them—especially that redhead and the four children—*but* most things I have are just for my pleasure, comfort, and security on planet earth.

When I signed up with the Lord, including the pledge card, I simply pledged to Him that I was agreeable to receive from Him the things He wanted me to have (read Malachi 3:10). He put it in writing to me and since He cannot lie, I figured that the best thing going was for me to sign up to accept all the good things He promises me on planet earth.

Throughout this book I'm going to be selling you on some of the advantages you receive *now* when you sign up with the Lord. I'll stress the now benefits because an incredible number of

Christians believe what Christ *did* for them in the past. They believe what He's going to do for them in the future. But for some reason, they don't believe He can do anything for them *now*. No wonder so many people can't get excited about serving Jesus *now*; they think He represents only future security, and their interest is in *now* benefits. We need to show these misguided people that Jesus Christ means tremendous *now* benefits and even more tremendous future benefits. This little analogy gives you a hint of things to come.

LICKING THE PAN

It's exciting to be with dedicated Christians, sharing their faith and testimony as they feed me the bread of life and share what Christ means to them. One such man was the late Dr. J. P. McBeth who taught at Criswell Bible Institute and from time to time taught our Sunday school class. By analogy he described how he felt Heaven was going to be. He told us that as a small boy his mother baked cakes for the family and permitted him to "lick the pan" after she finished mixing the batter. In considerable detail he described the joy of licking that pan and the immense pleasure he derived from the experience. When the cake was set on the table for serving, the rest of the family "felt" the cake was going to be a real treat. Dr. McBeth pointed out, however, that he had lots more to go on than just "feelings." He had had a sample. He already knew that the cake was absolutely delicious. Then, as only Dr. McBeth could do, he pointed out the reason he was so happy to *know* he was going to Heaven—because through serving Jesus Christ on earth he had already gotten a "taste" of what Heaven was going to be like. He knew Heaven would be like—well, HEAVEN!

I can enthusiastically "Amen" the pan-licking bit because my mother permitted me to "lick the cake pan" as a preview to the main event. Today, after feasting amply from God's smorgasbord on planet earth, Dr. McBeth is not only licking those heavenly cake pans, he's enjoying the full slice of God's universe with Jesus who went before him to prepare a place (John 14:2,3).

Now, before we move on to the next chapter, let's have another "snack" from God's heavenly smorgasbord. He keeps the serving line open all the time.

LOVE THE LORD—AND LIVE LONGER

Yes, I'm absolutely certain that Heaven is going to be—Heavenly. For a lot of reasons, as you shall see, however, I love life and want to stick around on planet earth as long as possible. According to the insurance companies, the person who goes to church regularly will live 5.7 years longer than a non churchgoer. That's interesting, because many times during those years when I did not go to church I would rationalize that Sunday was "the only day I had." All the time that was really the one day that was designated for the Lord. Statistically speaking, if you dedicate Sunday to the Lord and go to church, He will give you the equivalent of forty extra years of Sundays here on earth. Proverbs 3:2 clearly states this promise, "For length of days in long life and peace shall they add to thee." In Proverbs 9:11 He repeats the promise, "For by Me thy days shall be multiplied and the years of thy life shall be increased." This is scripturally verified repeatedly. We also have approximately 60 percent less chance of a heart attack and 55 percent less chance of a one-car accident if we attend church regularly.

SPECIAL NOTE TO MY NON-CHRISTIAN BROTHERS: If you are not absolutely certain about where you are going when you die, I'd especially urge you to go to church regularly so you could at least delay your departure, because if you don't know Jesus, you've got it better here than you will have it there.

THANK YOU, LORD

As you can see, after each chapter I am including a "Thank You, Lord" page. The top of this page simply says, "Thank You, Lord, for . . ." I don't know about you, but 98 percent of my limited prayer life prior to the time I dedicated my life to the Lord was spent *asking for* the things I wanted. It was a rare occasion when I said, "Thank You, Lord." I'm still guilty of spending more time asking than I do thanking, but the balance scales are changing.

In the newness of life, when your eyes are opened, you will see many things for which to be grateful. I urge you, at the end of each chapter, to pause and think about the things for which you are truly thankful. Write those things on the THANK YOU LORD sheet. Do this prayerfully, and the list will truly be endless; the eyes you used to read these words—the mind which enables you to understand the words—the hands you use to hold this book—the knees upon which you can kneel to talk with God. Thank Him for your belief in Him, and if you don't have that belief then ask for it. Thank Him *in advance* as He tells us to do in His book for the belief you asked for.

List all the things you are thankful for as they occur to you, regardless of how significant or insignificant they might seem. The blessing could be as big as salvation or as little as cream for your coffee; as important as the love of your family or as minor as the newspaper landing on the steps instead of in the shrubbery. (If you can't remember a lot of things to be thankful for, *you* really do have a memory problem.) The list will be long and important. Any time you get down in the dumps all you have to do is open your own "Confessions" and look at what you have to be thankful for. That, my friend, will raise your spirits considerably. (Then you can thank the Lord for your thank-you list!)

I urge you to do this at the end of each chapter. If you use one color pen the first time you read it and a different color the second time, I believe you will be pleasantly—perhaps even profoundly—shocked to discover that your list the second time will be longer than it was the first time. The reason is simple: As your positive confessions come forth, you will discover that the more blessings you thank God for, the more blessings you will have to thank God for.

REMEMBER: The more you thank God for what you have, the more you will have to thank God for.

First "Thank You" Date _____

Second "Thank You" Date _____

THANK YOU, LORD

FOR:

1. _____

2. _____

3. _____

4. _____

5. _____

6. _____

7. _____

8. _____

9. _____

10. _____

11. _____

12. _____

God is Lord of all,
or
He is not Lord at all.

Not the gold standard but the God standard.

Many times you've heard the saying, "Life is too short for . . ." and then the speaker finishes the statement by expressing some kind of truism like, "It's too short to be angry," or, "too short to carry a grudge." On the contrary, as my friend Dick Gardner points out, "Life is too long to carry that kind of burden." When you do carry a needless burden, life will seem even longer than it is.

The will of God is good common sense, and you will know the will of God when you know the Word of God.

If you don't know what God is saying, you will listen to what Satan is saying.

I recently took a torn-up twenty-dollar bill to the bank and exchanged it for a brand new one, which I promptly spent. When I turned the torn-up pieces of my life over to Him, He made me whole and assured me that the more I "spend" my life for Him, the more I will have for myself.

CHAPTER THREE

Long Faces—Short Pocketbooks

Concerning both humor and success, I personally believe it's Satan who sold the bill of goods that Christians should have long faces and short pocketbooks. After all, if Christians are poor and miserable, who would want to be one? I believe that God made the diamonds for His children and not for Satan's. Psalm 23 says, "I will dwell in the house of the Lord forever." He has the facilities of the universe at His disposal, so I believe He is going to build quite a house. I can't believe He wants me or any of His children to live in a chicken shack between here and there.

Periodically, some of my Christian friends question me about the biblical approach to worldly success. Occasionally one will even piously say he doesn't really want to earn a lot of money. In most cases I believe that a person who makes that statement will lie about other things, too. Obvious exceptions would be those who have entered some phase of church ministry on a full-time basis, a committed social worker, or a dedicated school teacher. I'm primarily thinking about Christian laymen who believe you need to have that long face and short pocketbook I mentioned earlier.

THOSE MISERABLE CHRISTIANS

Dr. Henry Brandt, a brilliant, dedicated, and witty Christian psychologist and successful businessman, often talks about the "miserable" Christians who come to him for help. Half-jokingly and half-seriously, but always in deep Christian love, he relates (no names, of course) some of his experiences in counseling. He points out, with tongue in cheek, as he lectures to pastors around

37

the country how when everything else fails they can always come to dear Dr. Brandt and he will read the Bible to them and share God's wonderful promises. He then reminds them that he is going to work with them by using what he calls "their" own book (the Bible). To be honest, I don't know Dr. Brandt's definition of a miserable Christian, but I would like to share with you my concepts about not only the three most miserable groups of Christians, but the three most miserable groups of people anywhere.

Group one are those people who have accepted Christ as Lord, who have known the joy, peace, and excitement of walking with the Savior, but for whatever reason—or excuse—have left the arms of our Lord and are dancing to Satan's tune. They "live it up" and apparently are having the time of their lives. They drink too much, laugh at jokes that aren't really funny, and change playmates or partners at the slightest provocation while assuring all who will listen that they are having the time of their lives. They change crowds and friends and stay on the go to the point of exhaustion in their effort to run away from themselves in their search for happiness.

Realistically, they will never find it because happiness is not a where or a when. Regardless of where they go or who they go with, they can never get away from themselves. Every time that "miserable Christian" looks in the mirror, he sees himself. Deep down he knows the thin facade of earthly pleasure can in no way equal the deep and satisfying "peace that passeth all understanding" which belongs to the one who walks with the Lord. I'm convinced that everyone who has taken a single step with the Lord is truly miserable when they get out of step. They perhaps experience some "pleasure," but pleasure is always temporary and constantly demands a greater "high." Happiness is a different matter completely.

The second group of "miserable" Christians consists of those individuals who read the Bible, know their verses, go to church, can quote the law, and are willing to "sacrifice all" and "die for the Lord" if need be. They are the only ones who are right and will tell you in a minute they are serving the Lord in the *only* proper way. They have a "cross to bear," but they don't mind. If they are happy, nobody knows it, and they give every impression of being weaned on a pickle. They are not "happy" in the Lord unless they are sharing their misery. Pious, holy, and sanctimonious, they don't believe you can succeed financially and be honest or have fun unless you are sinning.

From time to time I talk with members of this group, and to put it mildly, it is usually an "experience." About the only thing I can convince them of is that at least my heart is right and that by the skin of my teeth I might just make it through those Pearly Gates! We generally agree that it is only through the shed blood of Jesus Christ that we enter the kingdom of heaven, so we have the most important foundation stone for agreement. Generally speaking, however, these conversations are not very productive in that we are light years apart in what we believe it means to serve our Lord here on planet earth. Let me again stress that I do not feel I have any theological insight which others do not have. Nor do I feel that I have been annointed with any spiritual gift which is not available to anyone who asks for it. However, the first thing my pastor and Sunday school teacher told me when I turned my life over to the Lord was that the most effective method of "witnessing" was to tell others what Jesus had done for me. That's what I do—that's what this book is all about.

ACCENTUATE THE JOY AND LOVE

These stern, judgmental, Scripture-quoting (often out of context) Christians generally dwell on the sorrows of Jesus. I dwell on the joys. They stress that Jesus is everything; I agree, but add that He gives us, as His sons, through Him a tremendous amount of power and authority with a clear admonition to go use it. They believe in the law and judgment of God—so do I, but I believe even more deeply in the love and mercy of God. (Frankly, it's not justice I seek, but mercy.)

All too often they try to live by their own grit and determination (will-power) in God's law. The task is so difficult that these unfortunate individuals are often beset with numerous personal, family, business, and emotional problems. It's tough to carry your own problems, much less the problems of mankind on your own shoulders. My personal experience with these well-intentioned but sadly misguided people has been substantially less than satisfactory. They often want special treatment and are frequently rude and even bitter if their requests are not completely and immediately filled. Worst of all, they often take their personal debts very casually and often expect you to "forget about them" because, after all, "we are brothers." Incredibly enough, they are the ones who are the rudest and most demanding of others. In short, they are not following the simple rules of human relations as laid down by our Lord. No wonder the unsaved often look at this kind of "Christian" and mutter, "If that's Christianity, I don't want any part of it!" The interesting thing is that we, as Christians, basically believe many of the same things. The major differences lie in the degree of our belief and their conviction they are working their way in while I am going to get in through the grace entrance. Again, my efforts are to share with you what Jesus has done for me *now*. (All Christians seem to be in agreement on what He did for us in the past, and what He's going to do for us in the future. The major disagreement lies in what He can do for us now).

ENJOY GOD'S JOY AND RICHES—NOW

As I share my joy and *now* benefits—peace of mind, increased love for family and fellow man—everything usually goes well until I mention the men of the Bible who were financially successful (Abraham, Joseph, Job, Jacob, Solomon, and others). They grow more distressed by the moment. Once I mentioned a personal friend of mine who is one of the most successful and outstanding Christian businesswomen in the world, and who has been instrumental in leading hundreds—maybe thousands—of people to Christ. The person I was talking with and I really hit a conversational impasse. Despite the fact that the lady in question has given literally millions to further the Lord's work and has provided good jobs with steady income to dozens of handicapped workers, he felt she was "using" her religion. If *that* is "using" your religion, please, dear God, let's pray that others will also start "using" their religion in exactly the same way! If they did, we would have more people with fewer problems here and no problems hereafter.

I'm convinced that millions of people today don't know the Lord because of the long faced, poor, suffering little me, self-sacrificing, tell-everybody-all-their-troubles Christians who act like their second birth was just as painful to them as their first one was to their mothers. The salesman in me demands that I share with you and others the tremendous joy, benefit, and excitement of what Jesus has done and is doing for me now. Psalm 118:24 says, "This is the day which the Lord hath made; we will rejoice and be glad in it." That verse, beautifully framed, hangs over my desk as a constant reminder that I do have lots to be thankful for—*today*.

I literally try to reflect that joy in the way I say hello and deal with people on a day-to-day basis. On occasion, when people ask me how and why I always seem to feel so good, I will respond, "My health is good, my business is good, my redhead and the rest of my family assure me they love me, I live in America as a free man, and I'm going to Heaven when I die. Now, why shouldn't I feel good and be happy?" (Incidentally, whoever you are, you too have a lot to be thankful for.) Oftentimes the other party will respond, "Man, you are really an optimist!" Then I assure them, "Well, I am an optimist, but friend, you've got to face facts and that's what I'm doing."

SOME ARE CLOSE—AND YET SO FAR

To those of you who know the Lord, I say face the facts about what it means to know the Lord. Then you will do what Jesus told us to do in the parable of the talents as He separately instructed the two who had used their talents to "enter ye now into the *joy* of the Lord." In my mind there is no doubt that those who use their talents to serve the Lord will truly enter into the *joy* of the Lord *now.*

The third group of people who are truly a sad group are those who regularly attend Sunday school and church. They might even teach a Sunday school class, lead the choir or head a department in the church. In all too many cases they are even attempting to preach God's Word without knowing Jesus Christ on a personal basis. In so many ways this is the saddest group of them all. They're so close and yet so far. They try to obey God's laws without knowing God's love, and that is an impossible feat.

I met an ex-member of this group at a service station not long after I turned my life over to the Lord. This man was neat, articulate, extremely courteous, and went out of his way to be helpful. As we visited, he noticed the "Fish and Seven" pin. He commented that he knew what the fish meant, but was unfamiliar with the overlaid seven. I explained that the seven was to serve as a reminder to me that there are seven days in every week and they all belong to the Lord. Since I do not worship a parttime Lord, I do not serve Him on a parttime basis. I explained that I had recently turned my life entirely over to the Lord and that it had made a dramatic difference.

He lit up like the proverbial lightbulb and said, "I know exactly what you mean, because I just accepted Christ as my personal Savior and it has really made a difference in my life." He went on to say that for over fifteen years he had served as a choir director in one of the local churches but had not known Jesus Christ personally until very recently. At the time I was shocked to meet a man who had been in God's house several times every week, had heard literally thousands of sermons and testimonials, had undoubtedly read much of God's Word, and yet was living a spiritually empty life.

⟨☐✗ These beautiful gold-plated pins are available for just $2.00. *ALL* profits are used to set up scholarships to send dedicated Christians to *Bible*-teaching seminaries and colleges. Send check or money order to The Zig Ziglar Corporation, 13642 Omega at Alpha Roads, Dallas, Texas 75234.

At the time I thought this was an isolated incident, but since then I've met many people who are so close and yet so far, who profess Christ but who do not possess Him; who get in the Word but never permit the Word to get in them; who intellectually follow Jesus but who never emotionally get involved with Him and His work.

WHEN YOU KNOW JESUS YOU WILL KNOW HIS WORD

As I was putting the finishing touches on this book over the Christmas holidays, it was my privilege to witness to a young couple from Minneapolis. Through an unusual series of coincidences, they were in my home and I was sharing Christ with them. The young man had studied for the ministry but had been turned off by the hypocrisy of some church members. He had been publicly ridiculed by a pastor during a church service and had walked out on the Lord. Over the years, however, he had felt an emptiness which would not go away. Christ is everywhere, and once you've even had a hint of what it is like to know Him there remains a deep unrest that allows no real peace. He and his wife were seeking to fill that void so we were talking about the love of Christ. As we talked about the Bible and as I shared the things I will share with you in *Confessions,* the young man acknowledged an emptiness in his life. He told me that he had felt over a period of time that God was dealing with him. The result was that he and his wife bowed their heads and invited Christ to take over their lives.

How exciting it was to receive a call from him just three days later and hear the difference in his voice. It was full of love and excitement. He testified that since accepting Christ his whole life was different. He told me he had been concentrating especially on the Book of John and that God's promises kept jumping off the pages and were really a blessing to his heart. Incredibly enough, he testified that his theological training had not included the value of the Bible and the "now" benefits one could gain from studying what God has to say. Somehow its validity had never been tied to salvation. The young man was grateful that after years of struggling in God's Word he now knew the Author and could identify with what the Author is saying. That's exciting! The next story explains why.

INTRODUCING THE AUTHOR

A number of years ago the late Charles Laughton was on a Bible-reading tour of the United States. It was never my privilege to hear him, but I understand the great English actor read the Bible with such an eloquence that it was truly an experience for those who were privileged to listen to him. Once, at a large church in a small midwestern community, the audience as usual sat in awe while Mr. Laughton read from God's Book. When he had finished reading a silence fell upon the audience, a quiet which lasted for what seemed like a long time, though it probably lasted less than a minute. No one wanted to break the spell, perhaps feeling that it would be almost a sacrilege. Finally a little old man who must have been close to seventy years old asked for permission to read the Bible. The privilege was granted and the old man started to read. It was immediately obvious to the audience that the old man did not have the eloquence, the education, or the diction of a Charles Laughton. It was even more obvious, however, that he had a certain "something" the great English actor lacked. It was also obvious to everyone present that if this had been a Bible-reading contest, Charles Laughton would have finished a distant second.

When the old man had finished and the crowd was breaking up to go home, someone asked Charles Laughton how it felt to have been involved in such an occasion. With a wry grin, Mr. Laughton slowly shook his head and quietly replied, "Well, I know the Bible and I know it well, but this old man knows the Author. That's the difference." And that's what makes the difference in understanding God's Word. You must know God to really understand what God is saying. Over and over, He assures us that if we who are His come to Him in prayer, He will reveal His Word even to the babe though it be hidden from the learned doctor.

BROKE? DON'T BLAME GOD

If you *want* financial strength and security it is available if you will follow God's teachings. (I urge you to read the Book of Proverbs for the greatest lessons on business success ever written.) All I'm suggesting is that if you are broke, you shouldn't blame God for your problem because He wrote the Book on how to prosper. Question: Do you believe the Book? Jesus spoke to us very clearly on this point: "Ye have not because ye ask not." My Bible indicates that Jacob was a wealthy man, that Moses was probably a millionaire, that Abraham had "cattle on a thousand hills," that Solomon was the richest man who ever lived, and that Job wouldn't have exactly qualified for the food stamp program—if you know what I mean! None of what God says sounds like a beggar's down-in-the-mouth philosophy to me. Don't misunderstand. Money must not become your god, nor for that matter can anything other than Jehovah God. That's God's *first* commandment. Solomon tells us in Ecclesiastes that "He who seeks silver will never be satisfied with silver." We know this is true because within the past two years five known billionaires have died. All of them were actively pursuing the dollar almost to the very end. Somebody in Dallas asked how much money Howard Hughes had really left. The answer came back from a wise Christian, "He really left it all!" If anyone ever asks you how much you are going to leave, I urge you to tell them, "The same as Howard Hughes." Money can't become your god, but God can bless you financially and then use that wealth to glorify Him and spread His Gospel.

HERE GOD, TAKE PART OF IT

Over a period of years I gave thought to giving my life to the Lord. I even made periodic attempts to live for Jesus without letting Him completely have my life. For example, I would plan to tithe my income at a time when it was "practical," but somehow it was never practical. I always earned an awkward sum of money. Either so much that I certainly could not tithe on that income, or so little that even more certainly I could not tithe on that income. I kept planning to tithe, though, if I ever made the "right" amount of money. Obviously, no one ever makes the "right" amount at the right time under the right circumstances— as long as they are still holding onto part of their life.

When I gave *all* of my life to Him (admittedly, I keep taking parts of it back, but like Avis—I am trying harder), there was no doubt or hesitation as to what I was going to do about tithing. Besides, as I read Malachi 3:10, "Bring ye all the tithes into the storehouse, that there may be meat in mine house, and prove me now herewith, saith the Lord of hosts, if I will not open you the windows of heaven, and pour you out a blessing, that there shall not be room enough to receive it," it looked like a wise thing to do. We started tithing, believing God's promise but not because of God's promise. We tithe because we love God and want to obey His Word. What has happened to us financially since that date is incredible and beautiful. By coincidence, I pulled out an income tax return from the early 1960s and I discovered that my 1979 tithe and offering was greater than my income was just seventeen years ago, and my taxes are now far greater than my income was when I turned my life over to the Lord just seven years ago. I say this gratefully and to point out that the Lord uses the money for good purposes; hopefully, the government also does some good with the taxes. I must emphasize though that I tithe because it is part of my commitment to follow the Lord; it isn't a "business deal" with me saying, "Here it is, Lord, now give me the return like you promised." We tithe in faith and in love with the assurance that "all things work together for good to them who love the Lord."

LISTEN, AND GOD WILL TELL YOU

William Cook accurately observes that man was so designed that the only way failure could gain entrance to his life was for him to consider some plan other than the plan of God and some will other than the will of God.

I'm convinced more every day that God has spelled out in

minute detail the things we are to do in His Book. I can testify that the Lord is as good as His Word, that if we trust and believe and bring our tithes into the storehouse, He will "pour out His blessings" of all kinds, including financial. We started tithing as part of our commitment and God took our tithes and honored them. We repeatedly heard the phrase, "You can't outgive God," and found it to be completely true. Once, while figuring our tithe for a particular week, my redhead mentioned the amount to me. After a moment's reflection I commented that it couldn't be that much and that she must have added the income figures incorrectly. She rechecked and discovered that she had not deducted expenses, which were substantial since I fly a great deal. She smiled and wrote the tithe check for the larger amount as she commented, "Honey, we can't outgive God." I'll buy that!

When we start looking at the good things God gives us, we often forget that in Luke 6:38 Jesus clearly spelled out the plan. "Give, and it shall be given unto you; good measure, pressed down, and shaken together, and running over, shall men give into your bosom. For with the same measure that ye mete withal it shall be measured to you again." In a nutshell, it says that the big givers are the big getters, if your motive in giving is love, care, and concern. Obviously, if you give with one hand while expecting to take back a great deal more with the other hand, you have misread the Scriptures.

To me the message is quite clear that God wants us to prosper (III John:2), provided we don't make prosperity or money our god. In short, you can honestly get an unlimited amount of money, and there is nothing wrong with it so long as you don't let the money *get* you. I'm convinced that, everything else being equal, we can serve, witness, honor, and lead more people into a meaningful relationship with our Lord from a position of financial stability than we can from a position of financial weakness. (Please reread the last paragraph. Don't read something into it that isn't there.)

David tells us in Psalm 36:8, "They shall be abundantly satisfied with the fatness of thy house. Thou shalt make them drink of the rivers of thy pleasures." To repeat myself, I believe the Lord wants us to live a joyful, wonderful life.

To give you an idea of some more of God's promises, in Psalm 1:1 we are told very clearly, "Blessed is the man who walketh not in the counsel of the ungodly, nor standeth in the way of sinners, nor sitteth in the seat of the scornful." Verse three says, "And he shall be like a tree planted by the rivers of water that bringeth forth his fruit in his season, his leaf also shall not wither and whatsoever he doeth shall *prosper*." I believe that God is very clearly saying to us that when we walk in His light and in the guidance of His people that He sends prosperity our way. As a matter of fact, in Psalm 13:6 He clearly says, "I will sing unto the Lord because He has dealt *bountifully* with me." The Lord of my life does pack it down and run it over in all departments.

LISTEN TO THE RIGHT FOLKS

Let me be very specific. When I *really* read the first psalm about three years after I turned my life over to the Lord, I took another action which brought more joy *and* more prosperity. I engaged an attorney and a C.P.A. who were both born-again Christians. Although neither of these people bring any business directly into our company, I'm convinced that our business took the immediate and dramatic jump it did because God was simply honoring His Word.

We also changed to Christian suppliers on two of our major items and got better service as well as better prices, which simply verifies what God tells us in Malachi 3:11 when He promises to protect our gains from the devourer. No, I don't believe that I should deal with someone just because he or she is a Christian. I believe Christians, like everyone else, should earn the business or get the job based on ability and performance. Everything else being equal, I prefer to deal with a Christian, but I believe the Christian who trades on the fact that he is a Christian to get the job or get the business does himself and our Lord a grave injustice.

I suppose my pet peeve—or the people who provoke me the most—are the "brothers" who at the drop of a hat will point out my responsibility to them and tell me what I "should" do for them because, after all, they are my "brothers." It's especially disturbing to see anyone who thinks that all we have to do is "trust the Lord" for all our needs. I love what author William A. Ward said along these lines: "God gives us the ingredients for our daily bread, but He expects us to do the baking." In short, those who sit down on their faith and think the Lord is going to serve them on a silver platter are not reading *all* the Scriptures. God expects—make that *requires*—us to do our best with what we have. He is not going to be the whole ballgame (though He obviously could be). God is going to be the difference in winning or losing, but you've got to get into the game if you expect God to make that difference.

ALL IT TAKES IS ALL

God has proved ten thousand times that it doesn't take much of a man or much of a woman to succeed, be happy, and do His work. All it takes is *all* of that person, plus God, and the victory is guaranteed in advance. However, God wants our total commitment. In Revelation 3:15-16, He says, "I would thou wert hot or cold, so then because thou art lukewarm and neither cold nor hot, I will spew thee out of my mouth."

If a person really wants to succeed, he should remember the beautiful quote of Ethel Waters who said, "God don't sponsor no flops." In her beautiful eloquence, she also said, "I've packed my spiritual suitcase and I know where I'm going." As you probably know, Ethel has now taken that trip and unpacked her suitcase. She's Home forever.

YOU CAN'T DO IT, ZIG

I hate to be negative. As a matter of fact, I won't be negative. I'll be like the little boy who came home from school and said, "Dad, I'm afraid I flunked the arithmetic test." His dad said, "Son, that's negative—be positive." The boy responded, "Okay, Dad, I'm positive I flunked that arithmetic test!"

I, too, am being positive when I say that for years I periodically tried to lead a life in my own strength and will so that the

Lord would be "proud of me" for what I was doing and the way I was living. I failed every time, and with each failure I became even more convinced that I would never be able to live a Christian life. Obviously, I was right because my own strength and will was simply no match for Satan's. It still is not, nor is yours, nor is anyone else's. But just as Paul in his letter to the Philippians wrote, "I can do all things through Christ Who strengtheneth me," so can anyone who claims the promise of Jesus Christ. He explains in John 15:5-7 that He is the vine, that we are the branches, that of ourselves we can do nothing, but through Him, just ask, believing, and it shall be done. That's exciting. Serving Jesus Christ is the most exciting experience any human being could ever have.

IT BELONGS TO THE LORD

Occasionally I see some good Christian brother stick his chin out, pull his stomach in, and bravely testify that he's going to start giving the Lord 10 percent of his income. He does this with the all too familiar "self-sacrificing, what-a-good-fellow-I-am" look. Just to keep the record straight, this little story clarifies ownership in a hurry and lets us know who's giving, or has given, what to whom.

A minister preached a sermon along the lines that everything belongs to the Lord. An old farmer skeptically sat in the congregation, listening to but not agreeing with the sermon. That afternoon he invited the preacher to Sunday dinner with him and his family. After dinner they walked outside; the farmer made a point of showing the preacher around his house, barns, tool sheds, and pointed to his beautiful, well-kept farm. Then he asked the preacher, half-seriously, half-jokingly, "Preacher, I worked all of my life on this land. Do you mean to tell me that it's not my land, that it's the Lord's land?" The minister reflected for a moment and then quietly said to the farmer, "Ask me the same question a hundred years from now."

Yes, everything does belong to the Lord, and when we bring our tithes into the storehouse we simply are returning a tenth of what is already God's. The interesting thing is that most Christians who are serious about serving the Lord are very familiar with Malachi 3:10, which promises us that if we will bring our tithes into the storehouse He will open the windows of heaven and pour out blessings which our storehouses cannot receive. Incredibly enough, many of these same Christians do not read the next verse, which to me has been a truly great blessing. In the eleventh verse God promises us that He then will protect our gain from the devourer—in short, He won't let Satan get it! To me, this is especially significant because I've always had the ability to make money, but it always slipped through my fingers. However, when I started trusting the Lord in everything, including His ability to protect my gain, the results have been financially beautiful. Periodically during those frustrating years of my own roller coaster life I would ask the Lord to work His special miracle on me and change me for the better—*right now.* I never could understand why He didn't go ahead and do the things He claimed He could do until I read a little pamphlet.

YOU MUST BE "OWNED" TO BE CHANGED

Let's "hitch-hike" for a moment on Robert Boyd Munger's beautiful pamphlet, "My Heart—Christ's Home" (Intervarsity Press), as he explains what we must do before Jesus will change us. If you were invited to house-sit (stay in a house to look after it while the owners were away) you could not make any substantial changes in the house while you were there because the house would not belong to you. Even if you found the color of the paint highly objectionable and didn't like the floorplan or the way the furniture was arranged, you could do nothing about it because the house would not be yours.

The Holy Spirit is in the same position. He might not like a thousand different things you do, but there is nothing He can do about them, even if you ask Him to, if He doesn't own you. God simply does not change what He does not own. Now, if the owner of that house turned it over to you, then you could change it to your heart's content. You could change it completely, making it exactly like you wanted it. That's what Jesus, through His Holy Spirit, can do for you. When you "sell out to Jesus," turn your life completely over to Him and give Him total ownership, He will make you like He wants you. Then both of you will like you better. You will truly be changed.

ANOTHER EXCITING ENTREE FROM GOD'S HEAVENLY SMORGASBORD

It seems that people jet all over the world seeking happiness. They seek one thrill after another. They seek every form of recreation and commit every sin known to man and are still miserable, or they are miserable *because* they commit those sins. I hasten to add that this is more than just my personal opinion. Dr. Brian Harbour points out that Freud taught that it is man's sexual inhibitions which cause frustration.

Free man sexually, Freud wrote, encourage him to do what makes him feel good, and the frustration will be removed. This simply is not so, says O. Hobert Mowrer, a world-famous psychiatrist. After following the dictates of Freud for a half century, man is more frustrated than ever. Man's basic neuroses, according to Mowrer, are caused not by frustrations over the things he wants to do and cannot, but rather by guilt over the things he ought not to do, but does. With the love of Jesus you can remove guilt and gain the strength through Him to turn away from those things you ought not to do. With guilt removed, peace of mind follows and the need or desire for tranquilizers, pills, and alcohol are removed. This itself is quite a *now* snack from God's smorgasbord here on planet earth.

REMEMBER: The more you thank God for what you have, the more you will have to thank God for.

First "Thank You" Date _____

Second "Thank You" Date _____

THANK YOU, LORD

FOR:

1. _____

2. _____

3. _____

4. _____

5. _____

6. _____

7. _____

8. _____

9. _____

10. _____

11. _____

12. _____

*Your Christian attitude is contagious.
Is yours worth catching?*

On planet earth there are many kinds of people. In God's sight there are only two kinds. Not rich or poor, old or young, tall or short, fat or thin, black or white—only saved or lost. In God's Kingdom the mighty and the humble join hands where all of them become the children of God. Chief Justice of the Supreme Court, Charles Evan Hughes, and a Chinese laundry man joined the same church at the same time. That's the way it is in heaven.

You cannot be a secret disciple. —Romans 10:9-10

God has no grandchildren.

If you don't want to share, it's highly likely you have nothing to share.

If you are not living in the will of God, you are uncomfortable in the Word of God.

The Bible does say, "Pray without ceasing," but I don't see where it says you have to stop working in order to pray. As a matter of fact, I believe that anybody who can walk and chew gum at the same time can work and pray at the same time.

CHAPTER FOUR

It's "Good" for Them

As we would say over in Mississippi, I was "raised right." As a small boy, I was in the First Baptist Church in Yazoo City, Mississippi, every Sunday morning and evening for church services and Wednesday evening for prayer meeting. Mrs. L. S. Jones, from down the street, would stop in front of our house with montonous (I thought at the time) regularity. The instant she sounded the horn in that old Dodge my mother would say, "Let's go, boys," as she inserted the hatpin to make certain her familiar black hat stayed in place. We went without question because it never occurred to us that we had a choice (we didn't!) in the matter. Mama said let's go, and we went because she had long ago made the decision that attendance in Sunday school and church was not a matter of discussion or negotiation. She decided that her children were going to be in God's house on Sunday and Wednesday and there was nothing to discuss. She often pointed out that her children were all she had and she was determined that Satan wasn't going to get a single one of them.

Contrast this with so many parents today who fear (due to Satanic worldly pressure) that we should not influence our children by requiring them to go to church, that we should let them make up their own minds. One of the most common objections today is, "Aren't you afraid it will turn them against church?" I love what Christian psychologist Henry Brandt has to say about that one! He reminds parents that when their children are sick, they take them to the doctor whether they want to go or not because it's *good* for them. He points out that

55

parents are not concerned that the trip to the doctor will turn the kids against the doctor. Parents take kids to the doctor because it is in the best interest of the children. He says parents should take their kids to church, whether they want to go or not, because it's in their best interests.

I never understood how good it was for me until I turned my life over to the Lord five years ago. Here's what I mean. Many times I would protest to my mother that it didn't do me a bit of good to go to church and hear the same old thing because I didn't understand it. Mama turned a deaf ear and told me we were going anyhow. I even told her that I figured out things to think about while the preacher was preaching so it wouldn't be a complete waste of time. Mama still turned a deaf ear. To the best of my knowledge, I was sincere. I really didn't think it did me any good, which proves how much I knew. God promised us that His Word would not return void, and I can tell you that God cannot lie (like He said in His Book).

SO WHAT HAPPENED?

Those of you who know me personally, or who have heard me speak, know that I am a pretty excited guy. My close friends and family will tell you that when a thought or idea hits me I've even been known to literally *shout* with joy. I can tell you that many times I get tickled at myself as I speak or write when something good hits me. I'll say to myself, "Ziglar, that's pretty good." Then I'll grin at my exuberance but later—some times much later—I'll be reading my Bible and come across the very thought or idea I thought was so good. *Then* I'll really get excited and say, "No wonder I thought that idea was good. That's what God said!" Then I praise God again for giving me a mother who stood on God's promises and took me to church even though "I didn't get a thing out of it."

The value of this early church discipline was repeatedly made evident to me as I wrote my book, *See You At The Top,* which is a motivational self-help book. I wrote a number of things that I knew were right, but I had no idea where I had gotten the information. As I dig into my Bible and as I listen to people who really know the Bible, I am astonished and delighted with my scriptural accuracy. It really shouldn't be surprising to me, though, because I wrote that book the same way I'm writing this one—with much prayer, asking God to lead me and give me insight so that this message will be used by Him to draw people to Him through Christ.

THE CARNAL CHRISTIAN

When I went into the navy during World War II, one of my first steps was to move my membership to a church in the city where I was stationed. When Jean and I were married in Columbia, South Carolina, we immediately joined the church. We attended fairly often, but I'll have to admit that over a period of many years there were few Sundays I was really excited about going to church. My life was filled with contradictions and mixed emotions. As I look back on those years I understand much of the confusion, but when it was happening there was little, if any, understanding on my part. Even though I was active in some departments, serving in various capacities which would indicate a Christian life, I was actually living a double life since I pretended to be serving God while daily following Satan's dictates. My conscience wasn't too much of a problem, either. I'm alternately saddened and amused when I hear people say, "Let your conscience be your guide," because I can tell you with total confidence that some people won't slow down on their wrong-doing a bit when it's left up to conscience. Their conscience has been hardened, and they can do virtually anything without remorse or regret.

During those years of darkness I never doubted the existence of God. I just didn't know Him personally and largely ignored Him. I often prayed a strange prayer: "Lord, if You are going to take me, please give me five minutes so I can get my house in order." Now if this sounds strange or confusing to you, just think of how it was to me!

IT'S "THE THING TO DO"

Many people who know me fairly well will possibly be surprised when they read these words. For years I went to church because it was "the thing to do" and because that was the way I was raised. I felt a strong commitment not to dissappoint my mother who had lived such a beautiful Christian life. (Isn't it amazing how many of us work so hard in order not to disappoint our earthly parents—or even our friends and neighbors—and then daily break the heart of the One who died that we might have eternal life!) I will also confess that there were brief periods of time during the first twenty-five or so years of my married life that I caught brief glimpses of what it might be like to really turn my life over to the Lord Jesus Christ.

ANGEL AT THE WHEEL

One incident in particular was an eye-opener and should have been a heart-opener. Late one night while driving to my home in Columbia, I crossed the railroad tracks on the outskirts of town to take the back way home. I distinctly remember crossing those tracks. I also remember waking up as I was pulling into the curb in Fort Jackson with a military policeman in his patrol car flashing me down. What I don't remember is driving approximately six miles straight ahead and making a ninety-degree left turn at the traffic light, going two more miles, and driving past the security guard at approximately sixty miles per hour. Nor do I remember making several turns in Fort Jackson before the encounter with the M.P. who incidentally had to lead me out of the maze of streets I had just covered.

When I got home and explained what had happened to Jean (Sugar Baby), who has been my wife and my life since 1946, she smiled and said that she had prayed unusually hard that God would take care of me that night. Obviously, He had. There is no doubt in my mind that God had His hand on the steering wheel all the way. The skeptic will say I really was awake. My Bible says that God sent His angels to drive my car. In retrospect, it's amazing that I did not commit the rest of my life to the God who had spared me, but I didn't. As a matter of fact, if my memory serves me correctly, I simply said, "Boy, was I lucky!" instead of "Thank You, Lord."

THE FENCE SITTER

Perhaps I did not make a commitment because I was consumed with guilt, felt that I was "undeserving," and could not forgive myself for many of the things I had done and was doing. I felt I would never be strong enough or good enough to live the kind of life Jesus Christ would have me live. As a result I ended up walking both sides of the street at the same time. I cavorted with Satan's crowd and never dreamed of doing anything that would make them feel uncomfortable. I would have a cocktail with them and tell a few smutty stories (discreetly and in good taste, of course). I would occasionally make reference to the "Man upstairs" so many of them felt Ol' Zig was a pretty good fellow, even a little "religious," without being a "fanatic" about it. Then I would cross the street, piously adjust my halo, and associate with my Christian buddies while never saying or doing anything that would make *them* feel uncomfortable. The result was that both saints and sinners were apparently comfortable with me, and I was undoubtedly the most miserable man in either crowd.

While making my little trips between Satan's crowd and those who served the Savior, I obviously spent a lot of time "on the fence." As a matter of fact, I spent so much time sitting on the fence it was constantly in need of repair! In a way, I was like the fella who lived in Kentucky during the Civil War. He could not decide which side he perferred, so he donned the Confederate gray jacket and the Union blue trousers. This was fine until a pitched battle occurred between the Northern and Southern forces. Our friend headed for the Confederate lines, but all the Johnny Rebs could see was the Union blue trousers, so they shot at him. He turned and raced toward the Union lines, but all the Yankees could see was the Confederate gray jacket so they shot at him.

As I read my Scriptures today the words ring loud and clear

that the most miserable creature on earth is the fence-straddler trying to please God and man. He fails to do either and ends up not even pleasing himself much less his fellow man *or* his God.

THE "ALL AMERICAN" FAMILY

Over a period of years we gradually drifted away from regular church attendance, and by the time we moved from Columbia to Dallas, Texas, in 1968 we were attending rather sporadically. When we moved to Dallas all reasons for pretcnsc were left behind. No one knew us, no one expected us to be in church, and most of my friends were of the same persuasion, or lack of it, as I was. On the surface I was enthusiastic, happy, optimistic, positive, confident, outgoing, at peace with myself and with the world. I enjoyed a good relationship with my children and had a better-than-average one with my wife. As a matter of fact, our girls called us "the lovebirds." We professed our love, and most people who knew us considered us to be the salt of the earth, a solid American couple. During the first three and one-half years we were in Dallas we attended church only about three times. We were occasionally invited by the people I met in my work and my next door neighbor invited us quite often, but we gave the standard excuses and didn't go.

We didn't go to church although we would both occasionally, acknowledge a need and say we should be going. Both of our mothers would remind us when we visited them that we only had one chance to raise our children and they would be up and away from us before we knew it. However, we were pretty self-sufficient, our business was good, our income was good, we were getting along just fine, and besides Sunday was our "only" day. Additionally, I didn't personally feel a need for God. As a matter of fact, I was so independent and self-sufficient, I never talked to God about anything unless it was in times of desperate trouble—when I cried out in fear and not in faith. Incredibly enough, all of my life I had thought about prayer as a *last* resort. Nothing could be further from the truth. Prayer, as I fortunately learned, is our *first* resort.

As I look back, it's amazing the number of things I "bought" that are incredible in their inconsistencies and inaccuracies. I have to have someone explain it to me: God reveals even to the babe who prayerfully seeks the Word (I Peter 2:2). You can't have fun and be a Christian (that one rates in at least the top ten of the lies Satan has told). In retrospect, it defies belief, but, when you do not have a personal relationship with Jesus Christ, you buy a lot of absurd ideas because you don't know what He can and will do because of the love He has for His own.

SATAN'S SALES MEETING

Since I have been a salesman all of my adult life and have attended a lot of sales meetings, the chances are good I have sat in on some of Satan's sales meetings. At least my conduct would indicate periodic attendance. In times past, or so the story goes, Satan called a special sales meeting. In this meeting he approached his subordinates with a thought: "As you well know, our business is good and is getting better, but I feel there are some things we can do to lead more people astray. Our goal, as every Christian knows, it to convert more people to the kingdom. Does anyone have any ideas?"

At this invitation to speak, one of the little devils spoke up and said, "Satan, I've got a great idea. Let's tempt people with strong drink, except let's not make it strong to start with. Let's water it down and call it "wine," or label it with exotic-sounding names and colors and make it beautiful. Then they will not recognize the deadliness of the drink until its too late and we'll have them completely in our control. We will make it sound like fun, call it the "in" thing, dress it in the false garb of sophistication, and get athletic heroes to sell "gracious living" and fun through social drinking. This way we can subconsciously plant the idea that it's a sign of health and emotional maturity to drink. We'll even slip a real hooker in there with a slight halo adjustment and piously tell them they should drink only in moderation. Who knows, maybe we can even persuade some of the priests, preachers, and pastors to join the group for an occasional cocktail. Later we can even get them to use it in some of their sacred ceremonies."

Satan responded, "That is an excellent idea, and as you know, we're using alcohol extensively with devastating results. However, that idea about using those athletic heroes is 'right on,' and that wrinkle on moderation is a real winner. But we've got to have something else to go with that."

GET 'EM WITH GAMBLING—A LITTLE AT A TIME

At this point another little devil spoke up and said, "Satan, I've got an idea. Let's tempt them with gambling, but let's be subtle about it and bring it in under different banners. Maybe we can sponsor county fairs and have 'em knocking off milk bottles, poppin' balloons, and fishin' for prizes. We can progress from there and start having public drawings for cars, bingo games and raffles, all in the name of charity and worthy causes. If we handle this one properly we can even get the churches involved with the promises of profits. A lot of Christians still don't really understand Malachi 3:10-11, and they will figure they can cut down on their own giving. This appeals to greed and selfishness and that's a pretty strong appeal. Not only will this be profitable and an excellent recruiting device, but it will be fun to sit in church on Sunday morning and listen to the preacher as he sidesteps the truths of the Bible as it relates to morality and obeying *all* of God's Word. Actually, this will mean we've got that "preacher" doing our work, which really puts us in a unique position!

From there maybe we can establish state lotteries and even persuade some of the good church people to support them as the answer to the states' financial problems. (After all, it would be "hypocritical" to support gambling in the church house and oppose it in the state house, and the last thing these good church people want to be is hypocritical) After that it will be fairly easy to establish legalized gambling through horseracing, betting on football games, and the things which "people are going to do, anyway," so the state might as well be getting the revenue. So, let's sell that idea, Satan, and I'll guarantee you, with the element that follows legalized gambling, we can get a bunch of new recruits, because organized crime, pornography, and prostitution *always* follow legalized gambling."

Satan responded, "Well, that's interesting and you've certainly got a couple of good angles there but, you know, we're already doing a good job in that area. However, we need something new, because some of these preachers and dedicated Sunday school teachers who are spreading the Good Word about what it really means to serve Jesus Christ are making heavy inroads into our prospects. We need something additional."

MEANINGFUL RELATIONSHIP–REDEEMING SOCIAL VALUE

Then the third little devil spoke up and said, "Satan, let's introduce sex in a more subtle and different way. Let's persuade them that sex was created by God to be enjoyed and since the human body is beautiful, they should not be ashamed of publicly parading it. Let's sell the idea that in this sophisticated world nobody believes that sex is dirty, and because it's not dirty then obviously it's for enjoyment. Let's introduce a new phrase—let's tell them that the relationship should be "meaningful" for it to be acceptable. Let's sell the idea that pornography, so long as it has any "redeeming social value," whatever that is, is acceptable. Who knows, maybe the day will come when we can even get those nine old men on the Supreme Court to say (with a straight face, I might add) to the world that they cannot tell when something is truly pornographic. Of course, we'll have to hope they never ask a bunch of twelve-year-old kids what is dirt and filth, because they will tell us in a minute! Then we can expose through newspapers, magazines, television, and the theater the various acts of sexual involvement. Eventually the people will be led to believe that sex is fine with anybody so long as it is that "meaningful" relationship.

Old Satan grinned and said, "Well, as you know, that is far and above our most effective tool, and we're leading recruits by the dozen into the halls of hell through this particular means. We've done a good job of selling the idea that pleasure is a way of life and that the only way you can have fun is through drinking, gambling, pornography, and illicit sex, so we're delighted with our results. But you do have an additional thought there with the "meaningful relationship" bit, and so we'll put our best P.R. people on it and recruit some prominent figures who will endorse what we're doing. As an added thought to what you're saying, Little Devil, we will even get some of the churches, or at least they call themselves churches, behind the movement.

As an additional thought, we can start beating the drums for homosexuality. As you will recall at Sodom and Gomorrah, we really had it going good! And of course, in Rome and Greece and all of the other eighty-eight civilizations that fell, homosexuality was the final straw. We should start by getting a few of the churches saying that homosexuality is a 'lifestyle' and that David and Jonathan had a homosexual relationship. Don't laugh, Little Devil. We can get some of these good people—provided they don't read what God really said on the subject—to believe *anything* as long as we can get a celebrity to endorse it. This will create more problems and conflict than those Christians know how to handle! We can then get them in the public schools to teach their children (after all, there just aren't that many good people who have the courage to take a public stand).

Best of all, there are millions of 'good' people who will get so hung up on the 'rights' of minorities and the 'consenting adults' bit that they will completely forget that sin is sin— regardless of which sin is involved. Odds are good that we can have these good folks at each others' throats in short order. As you know, confusion is my specialty. Yes sir, you've got a good one! But it seems to me that if we're going to fill all our vacancies we need to have something truly unique."

TOMORROW IS SOON ENOUGH

Finally, a fourth little devil spoke up and said, "Satan, I've got it! I've got the greatest idea that has ever come down the pike. As a matter of fact, if I've ever heard of a bonus idea involving an extended vacation with pay, this is it!" Satan said, "Well, speak up, Little Devil, we're in need of new recruiting ideas." So the fourth little devil said, "Satan, I think we ought to do a reverse sell." Satan said, "What do you mean, a reverse sell?" The little devil said, "Let's take a negative approach. Let's tell everybody they should quit drinking, quit gambling, quit this illicit sex, quit embracing sin under any name." With that, Satan exploded and said, "Little Devil, you're out of your gourd! There's no way that we would tell 'em to stop that! Why, those are our most effective recruiting tools!" The little devil said, "Now, wait a minute, Satan, let me finish the story. Let's tell them they *should* stop all of those things." Then with a big smile he said, "But let's tell them there's no hurry—that tomorrow is soon enough." With that, Satan said, "That's fantastic! What a magnificent idea! Maybe we can even introduce a new or different word." And the little devil said, "Well, Satan, I've got two words I think we should stick with because everyone is already familiar with them. This will reduce our sales efforts while increasing our sales effectiveness. Let's talk to them about procrastination and use the most soothing word of all for the procrastinator. It's called tomorrow, and the easiest thing in the world to sell is, that TOMORROW is SOON ENOUGH to start." With that, Satan and all of his little devils agreed they had come up with a stroke of genius. Then it was simply a question of working out the details. The master plan had been formed. Today that master plan is working with enormous effectiveness.

Now, of course, there are those who would doubt that such a sales meeting ever took place. But, in my mind, not only did that sales meeting take place, but Satan is running training sessions every day, every minute, and every hour, selling the idea that there's no hurry. Yet our Lord tells us that nobody knows when He's coming again. The question to you, Friend, is, "are you saved or unsaved?" If, when you finish this next sentence, the Lord should come, would He claim you for His? Your eternal soul depends on the answer. We know that He is coming. The only thing we do not know is when. I hope you're ready when He comes. If you're not, at the end of this book I'm going to share with you some simple procedures which will guarantee that, regardless of when He comes, He will welcome you into His Kingdom.

As I read these words and think on these matters, I'm even more astonished that I didn't commit my life to the Lord before I did. There were those occasions when I was "half-a-mind" to make that commitment but it took a series of "weird" and "unusual" circumstances to bring it about. Before we look at those events, let's take a peek at a real "eye-opener" and sample another snack from God's heavenly smorgasbord.

HE'S WORTH MORE WITH HIS EYES OPEN

A little boy had six puppies for sale. They were cuddly, cute, and brand new. They were of mixed heritage, and the little fellow was trying to sell them for five dollars each with no takers, despite his big sign advertising them at that bargain-basement price. In fact, he had only one "nibble." A kindly man and his little boy stopped by and carefully looked the puppies over but they did not buy. About a week later the same man passed by and noticed the five dollars sign had been taken down and a twenty-five dollar one substituted in its place. Curiosity stopped the man and he asked the little boy why the dramatic increase in price. The little boy proudly picked up one of the puppies and said, "Look, Mister, they've got their eyes open now which makes them worth lots more!"

In the literal sense of the word, this is true for each of us. When we "open our eyes" and see Jesus as Lord and Savior we, too, are worth more—to ourselves, our families, and to our fellow man. Jesus loves us "just as we are." That's the reason He went to Calvary, but when we open our eyes and see His shed blood we are then invited to enter the serving line of God's Heavenly smorgasbord here on planet earth.

GET SMART—BELIEVE IN GOD
OR
BELIEVE IN GOD AND GET SMART

Many people I deal with frequently say they wish they were a little smarter. They explain that if they "knew more," were "as smart as so-and-so," or "had better judgment," they could get ahead so much faster and do more for their fellow man. One of the exciting things about God's smorgasbord is the fact that He puts the same items on the serving line a number of times. If you miss it the first time you can get it further down the line. The question is a very simple one: do you really want to be smarter?

In Psalm 19:7, God tells us, "The testimony of the Lord is sure, making wise the simple." So wisdom is obtained beyond the books written by man. For example, if you open your Bible and read the story of Joseph, you will immediately recognize that he did not go to a training school to learn how to run the pharoah's kingdom. He ran it according to God's direction. The Bible very clearly states that he was enormously successful. When we trust God, He trusts us and blesses us over and over. God tells us again in the sixth verse of the second chapter of Proverbs, "For the Lord giveth wisdom; out of his mouth cometh knowledge and understanding." James 1:5 says, "God tells us if any of you lack wisdom, let him ask of God that giveth to all men liberally and upbraideth not and it shall be given him." But God establishes a condition when He says in verse six, "But let him ask in faith, nothing wavering, for he that wavereth is like a wave of the sea driven with the wind and tossed." The problem is a very simple one—most people pray in one breath, "Oh, Lord, make me smarter," and in the next breath say, "But, of course, I know you won't." Now that's not exactly what I call a prayer, and it's certainly not what God calls a prayer of faith. So, if you really do want to be "smarter," ask God to make you smarter. He can and He will *if* you believe He will. That little "snack" from God's smorgasbord enables you to eat more abundantly every day of your life.

REMEMBER: The more you thank God for what you have, the more you will have to thank God for.

First "Thank You" Date _____

Second "Thank You" Date _____

THANK YOU, LORD

FOR:

1. _____

2. _____

3. _____

4. _____

5. _____

6. _____

7. _____

8. _____

9. _____

10. _____

11. _____

12. _____

Christian values are caught and taught.

CHAPTER FIVE

Come Into My Heart

I was working with a direct sales company located in Nashville, Tennessee, and several members of the team kept telling me about a marvelous Christian woman named Ann Anderson. I finally met Ann and heard her story. She had been in an automobile accident and her left leg had been broken in three places. Osteomyelitis set in and the leg became a honeycomb. It was not healing and there seemed to be nothing to do but amputate. After the date had been set and all arrangements had been made, one of Ann's friends pleaded with her not to let them amputate the leg until she had seen Sister Jessie, who was a prophet and an angel and could work miracles. Ann, in desperation, asked the friend to bring Sister Jessie to see her. Sister Jessie came to see Ann, poured honey and butter into the open wound, bound the leg, and prayed for her in the name of Jesus Christ. To make a long story short, Ann Anderson is still walking around on her left leg.

Not long after this, Jean and I were in Nashville at a convention and Ann Anderson took us to meet Sister Jessie. Our visit was enlightening and eye-opening. She said some things to me which were very impressive. She said, "You drink a little, don't you?" And I had to acknowledge that I did. All Sister Jessie did was shake her head and mutter, "With all that God has given you, drinking is really bad and you ought to stop it right now." The visit was reasonably short. She prayed for us and we left.

When we got back to Dallas we decided to invite Ann Anderson and Sister Jessie to our home. We flew them down for the Fourth of July weekend, and they stayed with us three days. It's interesting in retrospect to look at the events. As we analyze the three days, I recognize several things. Sister Jessie, may her soul rest in peace, was not an angel nor was she a prophet. As a matter of fact, she was scripturally inaccurate in some of the advice she gave to at least one of our friends. We have reason to believe, or at least I do, that Sister Jessie was possibly a little senile. However, there is no doubt in our minds that she loved the Lord and that the Lord used her to bring me, as well as my redhead, to a closer relationship with Jesus Christ. This simply points to the truth expressed in a beautiful cliché uttered by one of my Christian friends: God is far more concerned with your "availability" than He is with your "ability." Whatever she was or was not isn't the issue. She was *available*, and God did use her in my family's life, for which I thank Him. As a result of that experience, I sold out—lock, stock, and barrel—to Jesus Christ.

THEN THE GOOD THINGS HAPPENED

The things that have happened since July of 1972, make a tremendously exciting story. The Lord manifested Himself immediately to me, and I hope you will not misread any of what I am going to say. For many people, the acceptance of Jesus Christ represents a unique experience. Lights come on, excitement abounds, the experience is real and emotional. For others, it is simply a quiet calmness, involving virtually no emotions or feelings. In my own case I immediately knew that I was in fact a new man, that I was His, and that I would never again do some of the things I had done in the past. However, I saw no flashing lights nor did I hear any ringing bells. I just *knew*, and knew that I knew I was saved and that the Lord lived, and that I too would live forever.

After I made my commitment to Jesus Christ, my first step was to pour all our alcoholic beverages down the drain. Despite the fact that I was a very moderate drinker, we had a pretty good stock. Most of our liquor supply was given to us by friends and companies for whom I had spoken. The supply included a case of champagne, several fifths of Scotch and bourbon, and dozens of the individual bottles the airlines serve in flight. The next morning when my daughters walked into the kitchen, they were somewhat puzzled at the odor because it was much like a brewery. I know that drinking has no bearing on my salvation, but since God gave me my body and mind I know He is not pleased when I abuse either of them. Alcohol not only abuses, it destroys both body and mind. More importantly, my drinking would offend some people and I could not be an effective witness to them. Realistically, our neighbor might not read the Bible (he might erroneously think like I formerly did, that since it had dust on the cover it was probably dry inside), but, my friend, he is going to "read" you. For this reason the Christian literally becomes his neighbor's "Bible." When that neighbor "reads" you he needs to see there is a definite difference between you and the non-Christian. There was no hesitation in pouring the alcohol down the sink, nor has there been any real temptation to take a drink since that date—except once—and I'll get to that in a moment.

We went to meet Sister Jessie for the wrong reasons, and yet the results affirm the validity of the statement that all things work together for good to those who love the Lord. (At that point *I* might not have truly loved God, but my redhead did and God knew what was just around the corner for me.) We went to see Sister Jessie for several reasons. Curiosity played a part, Ann Anderson's enthusiasm played a part, and the hope that Sister Jessie could somehow wave a magic wand and bring us instant health, wealth, and happiness was undoubtedly in the back of our minds. In retrospect, I know we went because it was part of God's master plan.

For the record, I would like to stress that at the moment we went, my redhead and I were closer than we had ever been. My career was moving forward and the future looked extremely good. On the surface everything was coming up roses; but underneath there was something missing which is best explained by this little story.

THE HAPPY FISH

During World War II the government, for some reason, had a project underway to artificially reproduce sea water. The research was being done at the Massachusetts Institute of Technology. The scientists were confident they could solve the problem. They worked long and hard and finally one day the shouts of "Eureka!" or whatever scientists shout when they've had a breakthrough, came forth from the laboratory. They had placed natural sea water and man-made sea water under the microscope and they were identical in every way. Then one of the older scientists suggested one final test before they pronounced the project complete. Confidently the other scientists pointed out that the tests were concluded and there was no time to waste. The older scientist insisted, however, since the final test would delay the results no more than twenty-four hours.

The final test was simplicity itself. A barrel of natural sea water and a barrel of laboratory sea water were placed side by side. Several fish were placed in the natural sea water and they swam around quite happily (I'm assuming that fish are happy). Then the scientists placed the fish in the man-made sea water and (I'll bet you can finish the story, can't you?) almost immediately the fish gave signs of discomfort and distress. Shortly thereafter they were dead. The Master Chemist simply had not revealed all His secrets. Obviously, something was missing from the man-made sea water.

Something was also missing from my life but I didn't know what it was. As the saying goes, I didn't know what I wanted because I didn't know what was available.

NO, NEVER AGAIN

Now to the story of that one drink which Satan assures you "won't hurt a thing." My redhead's hairdresser opened a German restaurant which specialized in wines. We went there one evening to celebrate an anniversary and he, knowing the occasion, served us a small complimentary bottle. We drank it. We were hesitant, had some misgivings, knew it was wrong, but wishing not to offend our host by refusing the wine, we accepted it. When we returned home that evening our son, who was ten at the time, inquired about the evening's activities. In the process he learned that we had drunk the wine. Immediately his lips started to quiver. His eyes filled as he reminded me that I had said I was *never* going to take another drink. The sentence, though, that made me a lifetime teetotaler was, "Dad, I can't tell you how disappointed I am." No sip of wine or mixed drink on the face of the earth is worth disappointing my son or my Heavenly Father again.

I recognize the fact that many people believe it is perfectly all right to drink alcohol in moderation and that an occasional cocktail or a little wine is even "good for you." I'm aware that taking a drink or not taking a drink will have no bearing on my salvation, but since I *know* it destroys brain cells, adversely affects my performance, and could cause a brother to stumble, then I should not—must not—touch it. I also know that if I never touch another drop it will be impossible to ever have a drinking problem. Fortunately, I don't give up anything by not drinking. On the contrary, I retain full control of my senses (in my case I need them *all*!)

As a consultant I advise business people never to have a cocktail while discussing business. I do this, not as a moral or religious issue, but as a practical approach to being sharper for the discussion. For the social drinker who feels that a cocktail relaxes them, sharpens them up, and enhances their business chances, I point out two things. First you will, in the vast majority of cases, gain the respect and even admiration of your associates when you turn down the drink. Second, if you labor under the illusion that a cocktail sharpens you up, then try this yes-or-no, one-question quiz: If you ever have major surgery, since you want the surgeon to be at his very sharpest, will you insist that he take a drink just before he opens you up? 'Nuff said.

DOES CHRIST REALLY MAKE A DIFFERENCE?

YOU BETCHA! And that difference shows in a thousand different ways in every phase of life. Recently, the First Baptist

Saints in Dallas, Texas, played the Trinity Christian Academy Trojans. One difference was evident before the game started. The public address system went out in the middle of "The Star-Spangled Banner." The stands were packed on both sides of the field, and it seemed that most of them knew the words and the tune because they continued to sing and didn't miss a beat. How many times have you seen that happen?

THEY HIT EACH OTHER HARD, THEN KNELT TO PRAY TOGETHER

The game was hard-fought and the issue was clearly in doubt until the end of the third quarter when First Baptist scored two quick touchdowns on their way to an 18-0 win. The tackling and blocking was clean but hard, and the effort was as close to total as I have ever seen in a football game. The young men from Trinity Christian wanted to win as badly as any team I have ever seen and were as disappointed and heartbroken as any team could be after losing a "must win" game. However, when the cheering and tears had subsided, the young men from both schools were on their knees together. There was a total mixture of the red and white from First Baptist and blue and white from Trinity Christian, repeating the Lord's Prayer in unison. Then they got up and walked to the dressing rooms together. That's Christianity at its best. Only Jesus could have been responsible for such conduct.

If we would view things in proper perspective, I believe you will have to acknowledge that the committed Christians are, in fact, quite different. For example, in "Explo '72" which took place in June of 1972, something like 100,000 young people converged on Dallas. They represented every race, creed, and color, with the only thing in common being the bonds of brotherhood brought about by the shed blood of Jesus Christ. It is a matter of record that the Dallas Police Department did not arrest any of these 100,000 young people the entire week. Even more significant is the fact they did not have a single complaint. Now if you want to be fair in your evaluation and judgment, compare this with what happens at a *one day* rock festival or *any other* kind of event. Even as I prepared this manuscript a fourteen-year-old youth was stabbed to death and two half-brothers were critically wounded at a rock concert just thirty miles from Dallas. Don't misunderstand—I'm not even hinting that the kids who attend other activities are going to break the law. I'm simply pointing out that when Jesus Christ is the attraction, you will have a different audience, one that conducts itself differently. That, my friend, is a matter of record. My friend Sammy Hall, who was a top rock star and a drug addict before he accepted Jesus and started singing for Him, will "Amen" that statement all the way to Heaven.

ASK MY REDHEAD

In the last seven years I've had many people come to me after an engagement and comment that there is a new dimension—that something is definitely different and positively better about what I am saying and the way I am saying it. They can't exactly identify it, but they sense a new power and conviction which had previously been missing. They often use the words, "you are believable." One of my former associates, and now a friend and brother, was a little more frank. "You know, Zig," he said, "I used to feel you were such a phony when I heard you speak." Since he was right and I agreed with his appraisal, it didn't upset me the least bit.

I know Christ makes a difference because my life is totally and completely different from what it was before I turned it over to Jesus. My redhead would "amen" that statement all the way. The joy, peace, and security she feels in knowing that wherever I am, I'm in constant touch with the Lord gives her a sense of well-being that she never experienced before. The little things I do for her because I love her and so thoroughly enjoy doing them has made her a much more fulfilled person.

This closeness through Jesus can be shared by everyone, and the need for family unity has never been more critical than at the present time. In America today, roughly one marriage in every two and one-half ends in the divorce courts. However, in the families where God is on the throne and the husband and wife have the family altar and pray together daily, the divorce rate (according to Dr. Bill Bright, Founder and President of Campus Crusade for Christ) is one of 1,015.

> "Oh, what peace we often forfeit;
> Oh, what needless pain we bear,
> All because we do not carry
> Everything to God in prayer."

The couple which claims to have "tried everything" to save their marriage is inaccurate unless together they daily invite God to serve as their marriage counselor.

Jesus makes a difference in every area of life. As a motivational speaker I have been called many times in the past to, as they put it, "pump up" an organization. I was considered effective or I would not have gotten the assignments; but since my commitment to the Lord, I've noticed that the companies have changed the word. They now invite me to come in and "build them up." There is a difference, and the difference was brought about through the power of Jesus Christ.

Prior to my commitment, it had been a long time since I had prayed for anyone. If I saw a drunk, a cripple, or some downtrodden person, I would only think, "poor fellow." Today, when I see such a person, I lift him up before my Heavenly Father, knowing that the prayer is heard. My own life is blessed as a result and I feel a new sense of gratitude for all the good things God has given me.

THAT'S RIGHT, BOY, AND DON'T YOU EVER FORGET IT!

Upon my acceptance of Jesus Christ we started our search for a church and feel that God led us to the First Baptist Church in Dallas. We started attending a Bible study Sunday school class, taught by Mrs. W. A. Criswell. One of the first lessons she taught us was that we are not saved by feelings but rather by the Word of God. His Word reveals to us that Jesus Christ was born of the Virgin Mary, that He came to earth and lived as a man, that He was subjected to all the trials and temptations we are subjected to, but that He lived without sin.

The Bible tells us that Jesus died on the cross, that He arose triumphant over death after three days in the grave, that He lives forevermore, and that those of us who believe His blood washed away our sins will live with Him throughout eternity.

Even though I had been raised in the church and had probably heard it many times, it wasn't until that moment that I clearly understood that Jesus had faced exactly the same problems and temptations as a boy and as a man I had faced and would face every day of my life. Jesus knows how I feel because He felt the same way. How exciting to know that He totally understands my predicaments and problems because He had those same problems, and yet He lived a sinless life. He knows you and I can't do that, but He is willing to forgive us when we fail and fall.

Not long after the experience of dedicating my life to the Lord I was out in my swimming pool, looking up into the heavens, praising God more than just praying. (Yes, God had permitted me to prosper despite the fact that I had turned my back on Him. The reason is simple and explains why many non-Christians are at least financially successful. When you follow the principles and laws which are spelled out in the Bible, they work whether you believe in them or not. Example: step off the roof of a ten-story building and you'll discover in a hurry that the "law" of gravity works—regardless of what you believe.) As I looked into the vastness of the universe, I distinctly recall in my praising, "Lord, this is some universe You put together, and I know the day will come, maybe soon, when You will tear it all down." At that precise instant a star fell, and God spoke to me clearly and in my language, "That's right, Boy, and don't you ever forget it!" I never have!

I WONDER HOW THE LORD IS GOING TO HANDLE THIS ONE

When opportunities which occasionally come in the disguise of problems arise, one of the most exciting phrases that I have come to know and love is the phrase that my redhead so often uses: "I wonder how the Lord is going to handle this one?"

There is no question in our minds but that He will. When my redhead says those things, proving that she, too, shares my walk with the Lord, it rings loud and clear again that a real "helpmate" makes me a complete person. It underscores again why God so clearly tells us in His Book that we should not be "unequally yoked."

Some of the most revealing and rewarding things in my Christian life would certainly be considered insignificant by worldly standards, and yet God constantly uses them to draw me ever closer to Him and His love. For example, while working on this manuscript a simple incident triggered a series of happy thoughts. As we pulled into the gate at O'Hare Field in Chicago ending the flight from Dallas, the stewardess pulled a banjo from the carry-on luggage rack and playfully assumed the pose of a banjo player. I urged her to break out in song, but she pointed to the captain's cockpit and commented that she better not. Then I said, "Well, I would but I've got the kind of voice that prompted Mitch Miller to write me a personal letter asking me *not* to sing along (you might need to be over thirty to get the significance of that one!). Then I explained that even my own children ask me not to sing in church. In response to this the stewardess asked, "What does God say about it?" The question evoked a response that sent me on my way with warm and comforting thoughts.

MAKE A JOYFUL NOISE

About the second or third Sunday after we joined the First Baptist Church in Dallas, Billy Hilbun, the interim choir director, was urging the congregation to rare back and really belt it out. He explained that the psalmist had said, "Make a *joyful* noise," and had said nothing about making a *beautiful* noise. That really pleased me and gave me all the excuse I needed to really rare back and let 'er go.

GOD'S MUSIC

When I started writing this book, I had never realized the tremendous spiritual blessings I receive from music, but while putting my thoughts together, God convicted me of many things. One Sunday in particular it seemed all the songs were not only beautiful but full of God's scripturally-based promises as well. We sang "When We All Get to Heaven, What a Glorious Day That Will Be," and, of course, the Doxology clearly says, "Praise God From Whom All Blessings Flow." And then, "When The Roll is Called Up Yonder, I'll Be There." I'll tell you, those who have never experienced the total joy of the love of Jesus Christ and being surrounded by the voices of the believers praising God cannot even begin to know what a magnificent experience it is. There isn't a nightclub in existence that could come close to providing entertainment that gives the lift, the joy, the excitement, the pure pleasure that God's music gives. The Sunday we joined the church, the hymn of invitation was "There's Room at the Cross For You." As the lyrics were sung, "Though millions have come, there's still room for one," it stirred me to the depths of my being. The first Christmas after my rebirth Dr. Criswell told the Christmas story to children of all ages. As Ann Jackson sang "Sweet Little Jesus Boy" (my favorite song), the total beauty of God's love was brought home again.

Many times I can't join the singing when the hymn of invitation is sung and the pastor opens the doors of the church to beckon the lost souls to come into the saving grace of Jesus Christ. To see a small child openly trust our Lord, to watch a young couple rededicate their lives and their home to Jesus, to watch a senior citizen unashamedly step forward and invite our Lord into his life and ask forgiveness for a lifetime of sinning is too much for me. The tears of joy flow freely. Probably the closest thing to instant emotion for me is when Beverly Terrell, whom God has blessed with an incredibly beautiful voice and an even more beautiful heart and spirit, sings "Because He Lives." The opening words are: "God sent His Son, He called Him Jesus." At that point I can but shake my head in the wonder of it all. When Beverly hits the high point—"Because He lives, I can face tomorrow"—I just know all the saints from the beginning of time join in the chorus.

Today as I watch the choir under the inspired direction of Gary Moore, I realize more of the fringe benefits we get by coming into the church to worship God with the other believers. Talk about a place that jumps! I don't believe it would be physically possible to listen to the choir and orchestra give their version of God's choir and remain still. It moves and has a beat that no secular song can touch. Listen to a Christ-centered choir do "Battle Hymn of the Republic" or "The Hallelujah Chorus," and you've got to feel closer to God and love yourself and your fellow man more.

IT'S EXCITING TO KNOW JESUS

I was doing a series of recordings at about this time, and details down to the last degree are again vivid in my mind. I'm an exuberant, enthusiastic guy, anyhow. My redhead and I were back in our bedroom, and I was in the process of changing clothes to go to another recording session. In my exuberance I was taking short cuts across the bed. Since it's king-sized, I had to step on the mattress, which manufacturers don't necessarily recommend. As I was skipping across the bed I said to my wife, "Sweetheart, the Lord has really been with me on these first four recordings, and I sure hope He is going to be with me on the final two." Instantly, the Scripture came to me, "And, lo, I am with you always, even unto the end of the world" (Mark 28:20). Again I say, *Praise God!*

Sometimes while riding down the highways, either by myself or with my family, the full realization of salvation hits me, and I get so motivated I could almost shout. To tell you the truth, sometimes I do. I'm certain you have seen the little "Love Is" and "Happiness Is" cartoons, some of which are quite good. To me, love is knowing that Jesus Christ died on the cross so that I might live forever. To me, happiness is knowing *now* that my eternity with Christ is irrevocably guaranteed (Romans 8:35-39), that He did it all, and all I have to do is believe and accept His grace. As the hymn so beautifully says, "Jesus paid it *all—all* to Him I owe. Sin had left a crimson stain, He washed it white as snow." Yes, my belief in Jesus as Lord and Savior—and *nothing else*—guarantees my eternity.

AND I WILL DWELL IN THE HOUSE OF THE LORD FOREVER

Late one evening I was flying home from Chicago. It had been a long but exciting day and I was extremely tired. I opened my Bible to Psalm 23 which is so incredibly beautiful that only a loving God *could* have written it. I had memorized it as a child and had read it many times, but as I read it the concluding words, "and I will dwell in the house of the Lord forever," the full realization of a perfect eternity was just too much. Tears filled my eyes, and I could but shake my head in amazement that one who had lived the life I have lived would some day have the very best of an entire universe to call his own.

NOW HERE'S A RETIREMENT PLAN

Look at it this way. Despite the fact that we live in the richest country on earth, the average man will spend something like forty years working to support himself and accumulate a "nest egg" to "sit down on" during his retirement. During this work time he undoubtedly experiences some pain, poverty, problems, and pollution. He then retires and, in addition to the same problems, he often has the physical afflictions which are part of getting older. After working some forty years to retire, according to insurance company statistics, he will live less than fifteen more years. The intriguing thing is that he's worked forty years to retire for such a few short years. The same man or woman could spend just a few minutes on their knees asking Jesus Christ to come into their lives and they would live with Him in paradise forever. God's retirement plan involves no pain, no problems, and no pollution. They would have the peace that "passes all understanding" (Philippians 4:7). Like someone said: The wages are not always good, but the retirement benefits are out of this world!

On the other side of the coin we have the other group who confuse pleasure with happiness, who think fun has to be slightly sinful. They dance with Satan during their journey on planet earth. They are double losers since they give up the best possible life on earth (remember now, I'm an expert on this since I danced to Satan's tune a lot of years before I met Jesus) and the best possible life for eternity.

MAN ALIVE, THAT'S EXCITING!

Perhaps the most amazing thing about the Bible is the depth, richness, and hidden value which God will continue to reveal as we continue to prayerfully dig in. My friend, Bruce Norman, shared a little pamphlet which opened my thinking to an entirely new dimension as far as just the Twenty-third Psalm is concerned. You undoubtedly know the words: "The Lord is my Shepherd, I shall not want." But I wonder if you, like I always did, finish the sentence by saying or thinking, "I shall not want . . . for food, shelter, or clothing"? Actually, the Lord doesn't restrict us to those things—we do. Why not finish it as Kenneth Hagin does in his tract, "In Him"? "The Lord is my Shepherd, I shall not want—for love, for God is love. I shall not want for friends, because "What a Friend I have in Jesus." I shall not want for strength, ability, understanding, compassion—you name it, God is able." Man alive, that's exciting! As I write these words I'm aboard another aircraft headed back to Dallas. We're at thirty-five thousand feet, which is nearly seven miles in the air. I'm higher than that, though, with the love that is part of being privileged to personally know Jesus Christ.

To me, serving God is excitement beyond belief. Yet I know that there are many who mistakenly believe that if they turn their lives over to the Lord, it will eliminate all future problems and they will live a trouble-free life devoid of all temptation. Nothing could be further from the truth because the moment you turn your life over to Jesus Christ and start reading the Bible, Satan often enters the picture with a vengeance. He will keep you so busy you don't have time to study your Bible and set aside prayer time. Satan is a lousy loser, an intense competitor, and a supernatural being who will do everything in his power to divert you from serving the Lord. It's critically important that you understand that *you* are no match for Satan. Even God's archangel, Michael, was no match for Satan. When he had the confrontation with Satan over Moses's body he called on Almighty God to deal with Satan (Jude 1:9).

You can rest assured that you will have challenges and you will be tempted. But you can also have the complete confidence that in the end you, through Jesus Christ, will be the victor. And winning, my Christian brothers and sisters, is fun. Obviously, there is no way we can know what tomorrow holds, but we do know who holds tomorrow. As I said before, it's nice to know that you don't have to sit up at night and worry, because God is going to be up all night, anyhow; that we don't have to worry about tomorrow because He is already there.

DANGER IN THE PACKAGE

A few months after I turned my life over to the Lord, I received a package weighing about seven or eight pounds. There was absolutely nothing about the package that set it apart from any other package we regularly receive at our company. It was wrapped in plain, brown paper; the label was not distinctive in any way; the handwriting was not different. But when I picked up the package, cold shivers went through my body. I became highly nervous and fidgety as I lifted it. The thought clearly entered my mind that a bomb could be in that package. Now, I recognize that what I am now going to say will sound foolish, but since it is what happened I will share it with you. I was frightened enough to cut the label off and set it aside so that if there was a bomb inside and it exploded, we would at least know where the package came from. I say we because I obviously did not feel that my life was going to be snuffed out at that point or I would not have opened the package.

As I opened it I saw four absolutely beautiful books. As I looked at the print, the quality literally jumped from the pages. The titles were reminiscent of the occult or Far Eastern religions, so I immediately looked into the foreword and table of contents. I did not see anything that would explain my extreme nervousness, so I called our associate pastor and chatted with him about the books. At that time I was such a new Christian I did not want to put anything into my mind that could be in any way detrimental (still don't, for that matter), so I asked him if he would mind looking through them and giving me his opinion. When I explained my nervousness, he asked me some questions and directed me back to the introduction of the book. As we talked, I read where the name of our Lord was mentioned along with a number of "other prophets and great teachers." At that point I was able to say to the associate pastor that it would not be necessary for him to review those books. My decision was already made. After I hung up, my nervousness persisted, and I knew it would persist until those books were burned. So I left the office early and had a nice little fire. Almost immediately my nervousness totally disappeared. I'm convinced that the Lord entered my consciousness and made me aware of the presence of Satan in those books and emphatically told me to stay away.

SATAN DRESSES IN MANY COSTUMES

Interestingly enough, although the nervousness is of a lesser nature, I still have an almost identical feeling as I travel around the country. In virtually every major airport I am approached by members of the Krishna sect, a Far Eastern religion which is anything but Christian. For some reason, when one of them approaches me, I am again highly nervous. I asked one of God's very special people about this nervousness. I explained that I never have any inhibitions about witnessing personally or to large groups. But for some reason, as I am confronted by these people, I grow highly nervous. This beautiful Christian explained the reason was because they represent the thing I am so violently opposed to, namely, Satan himself. As I make the daily effort to walk with our Lord, I become more and more convinced that the closer we stay to Him the more carefully

He will warn us of any danger—including the presence of Satan.

This is important because Satan is so subtle (Genesis 3:1) that he often dresses in the righteous cloak of respectability so he can more easily fool the unsuspecting. The artist—under the direct supervision of Satan himself—who pictured Satan with a long tail and horns did a great deal to mislead a lot of people. Satan is far smarter than that. He comes dressed as an angel of light and is often cloaked in a good cause or charity to win the confidence of the unsuspecting until he, like the soldiers in the Trojan Horse, can work his iniquity from within. That's the reason God tells us to stay eternally on guard.

Although the example might seem unrelated, I believe one of the major lessons Christ was teaching when He fed the multitudes with the loaves and fishes was that when our faith is complete and we stay close to Him, He will supply *all* of our needs. That includes warnings and protection from those, including Satan himself, who would harm His children.

I'M GOING TO SERVE YOU, LORD, JUST AS SOON AS . . .

Deep in their hearts, I believe many people plan to eventually serve the Lord, or at least live a better life. However, it's astonishing the number of excuses we can come up with when the Lord begins to tap our shoulders to get started. It's much like the story of the three little boys eating candy. Well, actually, one of them was eating the candy—the other two were functioning as spectators. As the little fellow was eating, one of the nonparticipators suddenly said, "Give me some of your candy." The participator said, "I'm not going to do it. I was planning to, but you were greedy and asked for it, so now I'm not going to give you any." And he kept eating. Just before he took the last bite, the other little fellow said, "I didn't ask you for any." The little boy with the candy replied, "I know you didn't, so I didn't think you wanted any, and so I didn't offer to share with you." And he took the last bite.

Some people do have an answer for everything, and the answer is always aimed at their own benefit, or so it seems. The beautiful thing about knowing Jesus Christ is we learn so many of the facts about the abundant life. The Bible clearly says that as we give out, it will come back to us. If we pack our measures down and run them over, that's the way they will come back. This applies to all areas of life: material, spiritual, and emotional. The evidence is overwhelming—those who give more, get more.

Since July of 1972, when I became concerned less about getting only what I wanted and more concerned about giving to life what I could, I confess to you that the above statements have been proven completely true in every way. So, my Christian brothers and sisters, if you want to have faith, share your faith; if you want lots of love, give lots of love; if you want lots of happiness, help make others happy; if you want to learn the Bible, teach the Bible to others. The list is endless and so are the benefits.

BACK TO THE SMORGASBORD

As you've been "walking" through these past few pages, snacking on God's *hors d'oeuvres,* you probably worked up an appetite for some solid meat. So let's sit down to God's banquet table for another feast.

So many times people equate the dedicated Christian with an individual who is weak and deals only in apologetic approaches to life. In reality, the Bible is the greatest book on business ever written. Proverbs 10:4 gives sound advice when it says, "He becometh poor who dealeth with a slack hand, but the hand of the diligent maketh rich." This clearly says that we should not be careless, that we should not be weak, that we should be firm but obviously fair in our relationships. Business keeps coming up because in Proverbs 28:5 God tells us, "Evil men understand not judgment, but they that seek the Lord understand all things." Now friends, *all things* does cover a considerable amount of territory and gives you enough to eat on for a long time—like forever.

REMEMBER: The more you thank God for what you have, the more you will have to thank God for.

First "Thank You" Date _____

Second "Thank You" Date _____

THANK YOU, LORD

FOR:

1. _____

2. _____

3. _____

4. _____

5. _____

6. _____

7. _____

8. _____

9. _____

10. _____

11. _____

12. _____

Christianity is not a way of doing certain things, but a certain way of doing all things.

"For we walk by faith, not by sight." And, "Faith is a far better set of glasses than the believer has ever known before." "Twenty/twenty vision only satisfies until we know that there is something better." That's what faith is. Something that's better than twenty/twenty vision. — *William Cook in* Success Motivation and the Scriptures.

The Bible will keep you from sin, and sin will keep you from the Bible. — *Evelyn Vestal*

THEOLOGICAL DEGREES

B.A. — *Born Again*

D.D. — *Disturbing the Devil*

Ph.D. — *Past Having Doubt*

You can't trust and worry at the same time.

On smoking: Smoking doesn't send anyone to hell; it just makes them smell like they've already been there!

Today when I fill an occasional pulpit engagement, it's exciting to know that despite my comparatively limited knowledge of the Scriptures the Lord can use me to deliver His message if I will open my heart and let Him use me. It's also comforting to know that even though others might preach the Gospel better, no one can preach a better Gospel.

CHAPTER SIX

My Son, The Teacher

THE HARASSMENT COMMITTEE

I'm convinced when I made my commitment to Jesus Christ, He immediately appointed my son Tom as an harassment committee of one to make absolutely certain I kept that commitment. I'm grateful He did. I'm also grateful the Lord immediately revealed Himself to me in so many ways.

A few days after turning my life over to the Lord, I had a few days between engagements so Jean, Tom, and I headed for Corpus Christi to relax, swim, fish, and just be together. While there I got an exciting phone call, which again was a direct message from the Lord. About four months earlier I had been contacted by one of America's premier sales organizations to tell me I was being considered as the speaker for their annual international convention. I gave them my best sales talk, tooted my own horn rather loudly, gave them lots of endorsements and, quite frankly, felt confident I would get the assignment. A month later I received a notice from the company stating they had dropped my name from consideration. Frankly, I was disappointed, and in my own vanity (at that time I called it confidence) felt certain their choice would not be as effective as I would have been. On the surface I put up a brave front and explained to the staff and family that you "win some, lose some, and some get rained out." (I've always been a positive thinker!) Besides, there would be other engagements and maybe at a later date with the same company.

Despite the front, however, I was very disappointed. Then the telephone rang. It was the company which had turned me down earlier. They were calling to book me for that international convention I had tried so hard to sell. I'll tell you, I was excited as I wrote the date and location in my book. Then the Lord again spoke to me in my language and in clear and unmistakable terms said, "You see, Zig, when you leave things up to Me, I'll take care of it." Praise God!

I WANT ONE—RIGHT OUT OF THE BOOK

We spent two fun-filled days in Corpus Christi and decided to drive over to San Antonio to see the Alamo. As we started our drive, Tom asked me to tell him a story. I asked what kind of story, and he told me he wanted one from the Bible. Please understand that in Tom's eight years of life, I don't recall ever reading him anything from the Bible. I never talked to him about God, eternity, or Jesus Christ. It's not that I did not believe in Christ. It's just that I was ignoring Him. For this reason my redhead and I believe it was more than just a coincidence that Tom wanted a Bible story. I told him one and then he asked for another, and then another, and another. Finally, I said, "Son, I don't know any more stories, but as soon as we get to San Antonio I'll get my Bible and give you one right out of the book."

When we arrived at the hotel the bellboy had no sooner set the bags down before Tom said, "O.K., Dad, get the book." I got the Bible, turned to Exodus, and started reading about the children of Israel as they sought to escape from Egypt. I read and discussed the stories with considerable embellishment and dramatization. Finally we got hungry and I told him we would continue after dinner. The moment we walked back into the room, Tom said, "O.K., Dad, let's get the book out." Again we dug into the Bible and read until we all got tired and sleepy.

The next day we packed and headed back to Dallas. As we got into the car, my son said, "Dad, let's let Mom drive so you can give me some more stories—and I want them right out of the book." Let me hasten to add that in 98 percent of the cases when we go on trips, I am the one who does the driving. Obviously, God was using Tom to teach his dad a lesson. When we got back to Dallas, we bought *Taylor's Bible Stories* and read one of the stories each night to Tom. We started in the Old Testament and since those stories are quite exciting, a rather interesting phenomenon took place. Tom started having difficulty sleeping and even had a few nightmares. Jean and I decided that maybe the stories were too exciting, so we changed to New Testament stories for one night. Tom wanted to go back to the Old Testament, however, so Mrs. Criswell came to the rescue again. (Those classes are so much fun and so informative that Jean and I are scared to miss one for fear we will miss out on something really good. We know our hearts will be well-fed because we start our class every Sunday on our knees. We end each class with Dorothy Williams, the wee lady from Wales, praying for those in need as only Dorothy can. When she opens the prayer by saying "Our gracious and loving heavenly Father," you just know God summons his angels to listen as Dorothy lifts so many names in prayer. When she closes by saying "For it's in the altogether lovely name of Jesus we pray," you feel that God releases his angels to minister to those Dorothy has prayed for. The blessings we receive from Dorothy and the rest of the class are simply too great to miss.)

Mrs. Criswell explained that when you start putting God's Holy Words and love in your heart and mind, this bumps head-on into Satan's presence, and the conflict often causes unrest in the form of nightmares. She assured us that Satan could not stand up to God's Word and that the conflict and nightmares would soon cease. Sure enough, the bad dreams stopped in just a few days.

Once on an extended family trip I had a series of wild, unexplainable nightmares. After about the fourth one Tom, who was then ten, asked me if I had asked God to stop those bad dreams. I replied in the negative. Then he asked if I enjoyed them. When I again replied in the negative he asked the obvious: "Why don't you ask God to stop them?" How can you answer that one? That's faith at its most beautiful best. Tom then told me that one night he watched a scary movie (where was I when he did?) and just knew he was going to have a really bad dream. But, he said,

"I asked God not to let me have one and I slept like a log." Needless to say, I took my son's advice. I asked God to stop those nightmares, and He did.

GOLIATH WAS THE BRAVE ONE

As you can perhaps tell by now, I do love to tell stories and inject a lot of life in them. One night as I was reading the story of David and Goliath I was injecting some extra embellishments to clarify the story and bring out additional lessons. I pointed out that David's brothers were negative and afraid, that they figured Goliath was "too big to hit." David was positive and knew that Goliath was "too big to miss." They compared Goliath's size to their own which made Goliath awfully big. David compared Goliath to God, which made Goliath awfully small. Quite a difference!

Then my eight-year-old son became the teacher. To get the true picture you have to reverse the ages of Tom and me. Make him forty-six and me eight because the rest of the story comes off that way. As I was finishing the story I paused and said to Tom, "Son, David was really a brave boy to challenge Goliath, wasn't he? He was a lad of seventeen and hadn't even started to shave, while Goliath was a man of war over nine feet tall and weighing over four hundred pounds." Tom looked at me and said, "Yes, Dad, David was brave all right. But Goliath was really the brave one." Somewhat startled I asked Tom why he figured that Goliath was the brave one. Giving me his "Gee, Dad, you-oughta-be-able-to-figure-this-one-out" look as only an eight-year-old could, he said, "Dad, you've got to understand that Goliath was out there all by himself, David had God with him." About all I could come up with was a silent "Thank you, Lord," and a verbal "You know, Son, I never thought about it like that." Ah, yes, out of the mouths of babes. (I'm sure you've heard the story, but in case you haven't, God and David won.)

WE ALL MAKE MISTAKES

Not long after I trusted the Lord, we were in church. My son was tired and sleepy as the morning worship services concluded.

As we were singing the hymn of invitation, he put his little head into the song book. I gently pulled it back and said, "Son, Dad can't see." Once again he put his head back into the book. This time I roughly jerked his head back and said, "Son, don't do it. Dad can't see!" I immediately knew I had made a serious mistake as my son sat down in the chair and dropped his head to his chest. I sat down beside him, put my arm around him, and said, "Son, I'm sorry. I lost my patience and my temper." When the services were over we went back to our car. As we sat down I again put my arms around him and said, "Son, we sure know what we've got to pray for tonight, don't we?" He asked, "What's that, Dad?" And I said, "Well, we've got to ask God to give Dad more patience, because I made a mistake in treating you like I did. I'm sorry and I do want you to forgive me." He looked at me as only an eight-year-old boy could and said, "Shucks, Dad, we all make mistakes."

To me, that is the excitement of salvation. We all *do* make mistakes and our Lord knew that we would and will. He came to earth prepared to forgive us for our mistakes, asking only that we trust Him, believe in Him, and ask for that forgiveness. Then He not only forgives, He forgets. That's the Jesus I love.

BAPTISM—THE LORD'S EXAMPLE

I had been baptized when I was twelve years old. A number of people have asked me, as I have asked myself, if I believed I was saved at that point. As a matter of fact, until November 13, 1977, I could not answer that question. On that Sunday, Mrs. Criswell cleared it up for me. Chances are excellent that she, and maybe a dozen other teachers and preachers, had earlier said the same words, but this time my heart was ready. As part of the lesson, Mrs. Criswell pointed out that one way to determine whether you were or were not saved was the way you reacted or responded to sin. She pointed out that if you sinned without thought or remorse you could rest assured that you had never *really* known the Lord. At that point, I knew the truth. During the years after I had been baptized as a child I had drifted so far astray that the things I did were generally done without remorse or regret. When I rededicated my life to the Lord it bothered me that my baptism at age twelve had *preceded* my total trust in the Lord. Don't misunderstand. I know that baptism is not necessary for salvation; but, in every case in the New Testament when there was a conversion, baptism always followed immediately. Additionally, our Lord Himself was baptized. So, in order to get the record straight and remove this possible burden, I started thinking very seriously about this public dedication of my life through another baptism.

Two things occurred that really put my heart to thinking and would give me no rest. Not long after I rededicated my life, I received an invitation to speak at a week-end laymen's revival in Concord, North Carolina. Shortly thereafter, something else happened which really made me *know* I must be baptized again.

HE'S MY SON—AND MY BROTHER

My son accepted the Lord as his personal savior just a few months after my own rededication. That was quite an experience. When our pastor opened the doors of the church for new members, Tom told us he was ready. It was obvious to his mother and me that he was, so we encouraged him to act. We were grateful beyond words as we accompanied him to the front of the church. As Tom told Dr. Criswell of his love and belief, he was so choked up he could scarcely talk. I believe that had the most cynical, hard-hearted sinner in the world been privy to that meeting of an eight-year-old boy and his sixty-three-year-old pastor, the love of Jesus would have opened his eyes and melted his heart. Dr. Criswell has led thousands to the Throne of Grace. With his arms around our son, tears streaming down his face and his voice breaking with the emotional joy of the moment, he welcomed Tom into the family of Jesus Christ, and my son became my brother in the Lord.

In a few weeks Tom started attending the classes of instruction to make absolutely certain that he understood the significance of trusting Jesus. Our church does not baptize and accept children into full membership until they are nine years old. However, our pastor urges parents to bring them in front of the church any time the child feels led by the Holy Spirit to come and openly acknowledge Christ as personal savior. If the child's experience is real, and obviously some children have this experience at a much younger age than others, then this profession of faith in our Lord assures their salvation, and baptism is not important. However, many times children are overcome with the emotion of the moment or they are perhaps being unduly influenced by what some of their friends are doing. Since salvation is so important, Dr. Criswell wants to eliminate as many possibilities for error as possible, so our church waits until the child is nine years old.

Having agreed to conduct this laymen's revival the first weekend in February and because I had the burden of not knowing if my earlier conversion had been real, I decided to be rebaptized. My son was scheduled to be baptized at the same time, and I also felt that this sacred occasion would be even more sacred and meaningful if we were baptized together. When Dr. Criswell immersed Tom and me into this newness of life with Jesus Christ, it was and remains the most meaningful experience of my life. Today, I know Jesus Christ as a living Savior. I know His promises are true, that He has given me eternal life, and I will spend eternity with Him. It's comforting beyond belief to know that you never have to put a question mark after anything to which God has put a period, that you don't have to worry about tomorrow because God is already there.

"I ALWAYS PULL FOR YOU"

Two of my earliest recollections of childhood are the song "Jesus Loves Me" and the statement "God is Love." I've always associated Jesus with love and goodness even when I didn't show much love for Him. This incident, which took place a couple of years after I turned my life over to the Lord, expresses many of my feelings about love.

I love to play golf. As a matter of fact, there's almost nothing I enjoy more than just rarin' back and really bustin' that ball as hard as I can from the tee. (Then, if I can find it, I like to bust it again!) I don't play often because I discovered a long time ago that a fast game of golf and a slow game of golf both require approximately five hours. Since I average traveling nearly six thousand miles a week and am away from my family a large portion of the time, I have no desire to grab my sticks and head for the golf course on those occasions when I am home. But I do love to play golf. So, about five years ago, I came up with a brilliant idea. I bought my redhead and my son Tom a set of golf clubs. Everybody was excited about it except my wife and son. They both decided to go along with me, however, and we started to play. After about five games my redhead said, "Honey, you know, I just don't like to play golf. It's either too cold or too hot, too wet or too dry, or too something, so count me out. I think you and Tom should go ahead and play because you need to spend some time privately with him." There went golf buddy number one. At the end of the summer my son said to me, "Dad, I really love to be with you, but I just don't like to play golf, so count me out." There went golf buddy number two and most of my golf for the next couple of years.

While returning from dinner one night two years later we passed the driving range on North Central Expressway in Dallas. My sticks were in the back of the car and Tom said, "Dad, let's stop and hit a few." Well, my son is a smooth talker, so we stopped to hit a few. After a while he said, "Dad, let me borrow one of your woods." I protested and said, "Son, you are just too short. These woods are too long for you." But Tom insisted, "Aw, Dad, just let me try one." So I handed him the four wood. He choked up on the club, leaned back, and busted that ball about forty yards further than I had ever seen him hit a golf ball before. The smile on his face was the second most beautiful smile I had ever seen on Tom, and I knew I had a golfing buddy.

The most beautiful smile appeared two days later at the country club. This club has two courses for golfers and another course for the real old folks and the real young folks. We played the other course. On one of the par fours Tom hit a beautiful wood shot right down the middle. Then he took his five iron and busted the ball onto the green about forty feet from the pin. Now he was hunting his bird. To you nongolfers, that simply means that if he could sink this putt he would make that hole in one under par. I helped him line up and showed him about how hard to stroke the ball. He stroked it firmly and the ball went like it was tied to a string. BOOM! Right into the bottom of the cup. I'll tell you, the expression on that boy's face was the most beautiful thing I have ever seen. I grabbed him and hugged him and we did a war dance for about two minutes. He was almost as happy as I was.

Then I realized I had a problem. I was also on the green in two. I was about twelve feet from the cup hunting *my* bird. I feared if I missed my putt, Tom would figure I had missed it on purpose so he could win. This would have given him a cheap victory which is a substantial loss. I wanted to give it my best effort so if I missed I could honestly look at Tom and say, "Son, you won it fair and square." Since my best effort always includes a little providential help, which is perfectly legitimate even on a golf course, I asked for that help on this particular hole and got it. I stroked the ball firmly and it, too, went straight to the bottom of the cup. Before I moved to pick up the ball, I looked Tom in the eye and said, "Now tell me the truth, Son. Were you pulling for Dad?" Now I think you know what it would have meant to my boy had I missed the putt. He would have won his first hole of golf from his dad. It would have meant a lot to a twelve-year-old boy to win that first hole. But, without a moment's hesitation, quietly but firmly he said, "Dad, I always pull for you." Now that's love. Pure love. That's what we need more of in every city, town, and village in America.

When each of us individually, in dealing with our fellow human beings, can look them dead center and pull for them to do their very best for their own good, when we can pull for them to win, then we ourselves become more productive and more professional. When a witnessing Christian pulls—and prays—for the lost soul for the benefit of the lost one, the witness is lovingly effective. When the salesman pulls for the prospect to buy for the prospect's own benefit, when the sales manager pulls for the prospective sales person to join his organization for the sales person's benefit, that is the instant the sales manager becomes more productive. When teachers pull for students and managers pull for employees, parents pull for their children, and husbands and wives pull for each other, then that helps each person to realize his own worth even more. It helps them to do better. As my friend Cavett Robert loves to say, "People don't care how much you know until they know how much you care." But for them to know of your love, you must show your love. Pull for them by praying for them.

You demonstrate love, care, and concern by pulling for and helping those people you deal with to accomplish their objectives. That's the reason I'm so grateful that I know Jesus Christ personally. It's exciting to know that an all-knowing, all-loving God, the Creator of the universe who knows even when a sparrow falls, loved me so much before I was born that He came to earth and lay down His own life that I might live. Knowing that "God so loved the world that He gave His only begotten Son, that whosoever believeth in Him should not perish but have everlasting life," is a source of unspeakable joy and comfort. Knowing that this is the Jesus who is pulling for me and you is the most comforting thing in the world.

A MOTHER'S LOVE

As you can see, my family plays a big and important part in my life. Our Lord placed His strongest possible seal of approval on the family. As a matter of fact, one reason I believe Jesus Christ is God's only begotten Son has to do with a mother's love. The love that Mary, Jesus's mother, had for her Son is woven throughout the Gospels. Never was His divinity more evident than at His trial and crucifixion.

You know the story—the trial was a mockery; the mob wanted His life and despite His obvious innocence they would settle for nothing less. Surely you can imagine the feelings of His mother as He was mocked, falsely accused, scourged, beaten, spat upon, and finally nailed naked on a cross between two thieves while Roman soldiers gambled over his garments. Surely you must know the agony of this woman who had been entrusted with being His mother. Every fibre of her being must have screamed out in agony as she watched what was happening to the only perfect person to ever walk the face of the earth. Yet, it is an historical fact that not once did she raise her voice and deny Jesus was God's only Son, sent to earth. She kept still because she knew, better than anyone else on earth could have possibly known, that Jesus Christ, whom she had borne as His earthly mother, was God's son, that He had come that "all the Scriptures might be fulfilled" (Mark 15:28).

SMORGASBORD TIME AGAIN

This time as you go down the serving line of God's Heavenly smorgasbord on planet earth, God is going to reach out and *take* something off your tray so there will be more room for Him to load your tray (your life) with the good things He wants you to have. Now, I'll be the first to admit that God can't take this item—called worry—off your tray unless you permit Him to do so.

Many times people ask me if I worry. The answer is no, I really don't, because I confess that Jesus and not Satan is in control of my life. For those who don't know Jesus, I suggest a practical approach to the worry problem. First of all, you should set aside a certain "worry" time each week; for example, Thursday afternoon at three o'clock. You also need a special worry spot, since worrying is serious business. It also requires preparation, so I would suggest that during the course of the week you have a worry pad. As things occur which you know will require concentration, simply list them on a sheet of paper and number them so you can easily keep track of *all* the things you feel will require your best negative attention. I would urge you to list as many things as possible during the week. Many of the things you had planned to worry about will have disappeared and will require little or no worry, certainly not your best worrying effort. The long list will guarantee you that your worry hour will be a reasonably busy one. Otherwise you will probably worry because you have nothing to worry about. Then, Thursday afternoon at three, if anyone asks you where you are going you can—with a degree of indignation—tell them you are going to the worry room. Furthermore, you are going to worry "scientifically."

Ridiculous! Of course it is, but then, so is worry! Worry is stewing without doing. It's interest paid on trouble which never comes due. Worry, as my friend Evelyn Vestal tells me, prevents God from doing anything for us. Jesus tells us we have not because we ask not. Surely that includes faith, which is the opposite of worry. Psalm 27:1 says, "The Lord is my light and my salvation, whom shall I fear? The Lord is the strength of my life, of whom shall I be afraid?" The boozers and pill-poppers do so because they want to relax and get away from it all, or to relieve tension. Fear causes worry and worry causes tension. If you did not fear today or tomorrow, what would you have to worry about? Since faith is your reaction to God's ability and since God has the ability to solve our problems, He will be pleased to remove your worry from your smorgasbord tray—*if* you will let Him.

REMEMBER: The more you thank God for what you have, the more you will have to thank God for.

First "Thank You" Date _____

Second "Thank You" Date _____

THANK YOU, LORD

FOR:

1. _____

2. _____

3. _____

4. _____

5. _____

6. _____

7. _____

8. _____

9. _____

10. _____

11. _____

12. _____

God created man on purpose
—and for a purpose.

A statement made me marvel recently, "People are more interested in being religious than in being righteous." Religion and righteousness should go hand in hand. Perhaps this is why James added "pure" to religion when he offered religion as righteousness. Again, man is instinctively religious. He has this in his soul. But this is not the religion that saves. Actually, instinct and real religion are two different things. A sister said, "My religion would not allow my divorcing him." But her "religion" did not prompt her to be a sweet wife and work at having a good marriage. She had religion but not righteousness. — Charles Hodge

If you can't be generous when it's hard, you won't be when it's easy.

You can lose fellowship with God but not a relationship.

There are two natures in my breast:
One I love and one I hate.
The one I feed will dominate.

The God Who made you can make you over.

CHAPTER SEVEN

The Jesus I Love

As the Roman soldier at the crucifixion said, "Surely this is no ordinary man." Any fair-minded individual would have to agree. Ask ten thousand educated people from every corner of the globe to name the ten greatest men who ever lived and you would surely get ten thousand different lists. Ask them to name *the* greatest man who ever lived and the result would be a foregone conclusion. Jesus Christ. The reason again is obvious to any fair-minded person. He was no ordinary man. He was and is our Lord. He put aside His mantle of Deity and came down to earth as our redeemer. He lived as a man, was subjected to *every* temptation you and I are subjected to, yet he lived without sin, which *no* mortal could possibly do. Time in the civilized world is measured by His birth. It's either B.C. or A.D. This is proper because He is alpha and omega—the beginning and the end. Bishop Phillips Brooks said it simply and beautifully in his "One Solitary Life."

ONE SOLITARY LIFE

He was born in an obscure village, the child of a peasant woman. Until He was thirty He worked in a carpenter shop, and then for three years He was an itinerant preacher.

He wrote no books. He held no office. He never owned a home. He was never in a big city. He never traveled two hundred miles from the place where He was born. He never did one of the things that usually accompany greatness.

The authorities condemned His teachings. His friends deserted Him. One betrayed Him to His enemies for a paltry sum. One denied Him. He went through the mockery of a trial. He was nailed upon a cross between two thieves. While He was dying His executioners gambled for the only piece of property He owned on Earth—His coat. When He was dead He was taken down and laid in a borrowed grave.

Nineteen wide centuries have come and gone, yet today He is the crowning glory of the human race, the adored leader of millions of the Earth's inhabitants.

All the armies that ever marched and all the navies that were ever built and all the parliaments that ever sat and all the rulers that ever reigned—put together—have not affected the life of man upon this Earth so profoundly as that One Solitary Life!

KEEP YOUR EYES ON THE LORD

Now my Christian brother or sister, let me urge you to read and remember the story of the Apostle Peter in Matthew 14:25-31. In this story our Lord is walking across the water to the ship where His disciples are fishing. Peter, the impetuous one, asked for permission to do the same thing. Our Lord simply said, "Come," and Peter confidently stepped out of the ship onto the water and started walking toward Jesus. Then the Scriptures say, "But when he saw the wind boisterous, he was afraid." At that instant he started to sink but Jesus reached down and lifted him up. There are two important messages here. First, Peter would not have seen the wind if he had kept his eyes on Jesus. Secondly, the instant he got into trouble he acknowledged his helplessness, asked for help, and Christ lifted him up. Keep your eyes on Jesus and know that He is always ready and able to help. That's the Jesus I love. That's the Jesus we need to keep our eyes on.

From time to time I hear people say that at one time they followed the Lord and were active in church and Christian activities. When I press them for details they will often tell me about some extreme disappointment they experienced in a certain person whom they idolized. Invariably it is a person in a leadership position in a Christian group who turned out to be less than genuine. How tragic! Two thoughts: first, we should never idolize any person. If we do, we are doomed to disappointment. We must keep our eyes on *Jesus*, and then we won't be disappointed. This is as true today as it was in the beginning and throughout the history of the Bible. Abraham was a good man with much faith, but he was a colossal liar who laughed when God told him at age ninety-nine he would father a great nation. Jacob was a conniver of the first order. His very name means "supplanter." David was a man after God's own heart, but he was an adulterous murderer. Peter was a dogmatic and outspoken disciple, but he profanely denied our Lord. Even Paul, the greatest Christian writer and theologian of all time, had such a violent argument with Barnabas that each went his separate way. The list, both past and present, goes on and on and will never end. I say it again and yet again: don't look up to any mortal and expect perfection because it simply isn't there. If you do you will ultimately be disappointed. Again I say: keep your eyes on Jesus and only on Jesus and there will be no disappointment.

Second thought: since people often draw the wrong conclusions about others, it is mandatory for Christians to constantly walk with the Lord and to be careful not to give anyone the wrong impression with the appearance of wrong-doing. Here's what I mean.

SHE SURE ENJOYS HER DRINKS

Not long after I committed my life to the Lord, I was on a speaking engagement in Springfield, Missouri. After the engagement I was having a conversation with an executive from a manufacturing company. I was witnessing on the importance of serving Christ seven days a week and not just on Sunday. (I'm personally convinced that those who "religiously" show up on Sunday morning for their public halo adjustment, and then make no effort to live for Christ the other six days of the week, are one of Satan's most effective tools.) My newly found acquaintance mentioned the fact that a good friend of mine who professed the same thing was guilty of imbibing or, as he put it, "She sure enjoys her drinks," and didn't I think she was being hypocritical? Since I knew the lady in question quite well, I immediately challenged him on the subject. I know her total, deep, and long-lasting Christian commitment, so I assured him there was no way she would consider drinking any alcoholic beverage. He then told me he had personally seen her with a drink in her hands. I then asked, "Are you certain it was alcohol, or could it have been a Coke or Seven-Up?" He admitted that it could easily have been a soft drink. Later he confessed that on second thought he was sure it was something other than booze. There are two lessons to be learned from this incident. One, we should be extremely careful about observations we make about others because the chances of a wrong accusation are great. Two, as Christians, we must be especially careful that what we do does not even *appear* to be evil.

My business involvement often takes me to cocktail parties or into situations where drinks are served, but after this incident, I resolved to be extremely careful to avoid even "the appearance of evil." Since that date I am careful not to drink a Coke or Seven-Up where liquor is being served for fear that some Christian brother who is seriously considering a total commitment to the Lord might draw the wrong conclusion. To some of you, especially those who do not know the Lord, this might sound a bit stuffy. If it does, please be assured that I much prefer you think I'm stuffy than that I, through ignorance or carelessness, would cause some "little one" in the faith to pause or stumble.

Once I expressed this concern to a magazine writer during an interview. He was shocked and then dismayed when I elaborated by saying that I was careful not to even have coffee with a member of the opposite sex. He really thought I was "way out" when I observed that I would never take my secretary to lunch. The reason as I explained it to him is simple. First of all, I have nothing to discuss with my secretary (or any other member of the opposite sex) which I could not discuss in the office. Secondly, if I avoid a situation which *could* be misinterpreted by *anyone*, then I feel I'm ahead of the game.

The reporter in question, a pleasant young man, apparently felt this approach was either phony or far-fetched because he never printed the interview. Don't feel too sorry for me for losing the publicity from his one hundred thousand subscription edition though, because immediately thereafter the Lord replaced it with an article in *Guideposts,* which has twelve million readers. I assume it was the Lord because that's the way He generally does things.

THEY JUDGE US DIFFERENTLY

Those who don't know Jesus look at us who claim Him as Lord and expect us to be different. Just one slip or indication of anything less than a perfect Christian performance, and we are open to criticism. In a way, it's difficult to understand why anyone would think only perfect people, or for that matter only Christians, go to Christian churches. Going to church, regardless of how often you go, doesn't make you a Christian any more than going to a garage, regardless of how long you stay, will make you an automobile. Everyone knows you build a hospital for the folks who are sick, not for those who are well. Why should they think that the church is a home for only the perfect? It's a place for sinners to worship and seek a closer, more meaningful relationship with Christ. No, Christians are not perfect, but they are saved and that's the important thing.

Yes, the world does judge us by different standards, and I praise God for this fact because Christians *are* different. For example, you could walk down any street in the U.S. with a case of beer or a couple of bottles of booze under your arm and most people would smile and comment, "Looks like somebody is going to have a good time tonight." Most of them would see nothing wrong with it, nor would they make any critical comments. Yet when a Christian walks down the same street with a Bible under his arm and the love of Jesus Christ showing in his eyes, many of the same people would say, "I wonder what that kook is up to?" At this point I think it is critical that we understand that even though they might be criticizing you and ridiculing you publicly, they are often secretly envious and admire you greatly. The Anita Bryant story clearly proves the point. The question is, how do Americans and the world—despite media coverage to the contrary—really feel about Anita Bryant? The answer, according to a recently concluded *Good Housekeeping* poll, is that Anita Bryant is the most admired woman in the world.

ANITA BRYANT

As most of you who are reading this book know, Anita Bryant has been fighting a costly, bitter, and until now, very lonely battle. She's fought with force and conviction as well as love and has stayed completely within the law. I'm speaking of her outspoken stand against homosexuality and the battle which she fought, and almost single-handedly won (though she would deny this as being an individual effort), to keep homosexuals from teaching the school children in Dade County, Florida. This battle has been waged at great personal sacrifice because it has cost her a number of personal appearances which are a prime source of income for her. The homosexual community has boycotted Florida orange juice and exerted extreme pressure to get her dropped from television commercials. Additionally, many guests of various talk shows have refused to appear on shows with her, which also reduces her income because it reduces her appearances.

I just praise God that we have people like Anita and her husband, Bob Green, who supports her all the way. Despite the bitterness of the attacks and the physical threats on their lives, Anita and Bob stake their future and stand their ground on what they believe. A recent incident reveals more than anything else the effect Jesus Christ has on the life of Anita Bryant and her husband.

Bob and Anita were at a news conference responding to media questions when a homosexual picked up a pie and threw it in Anita's face. I think it's safe to say that 999 people out of a thousand would have reacted violently. A crowd did immediately gather and a serious incident could well have been in the making. But Bob Green, a big, husky guy who probably could have obliterated the homosexual, very quietly but firmly said, "No, leave him alone." They did not press charges. They did not have him arrested, although this physical attack would have undoubtedly put the homosexual in a very serious position. The question is then, what did Bob and Anita do? The answer: they quietly bowed their heads and prayed for the homosexual. They asked God to let the homosexual know they loved him as a person but hated the sin of homosexuality. All of this took place with the flash bulbs and the T.V. cameras going full speed. *That* is Jesus Christ—that is the Lord I love, the One who can make a human's heart like that.

TUNE IN FOR A CHANGE

Many homosexuals say they were "born that way," and some Christians, who of all people should know better, agree with them. Even a casual reading of the Bible reveals the fallacy of this thinking. Leviticus 20:13 clearly points out that homosexuality is a sin unto death. Surely any thinking Christian would know that an all-loving God would not make a person a homosexual and then kill him for being one. The latest Masters and Johnson study clearly established that homosexuality is a *learned* or *acquired habit.* They were successful in bringing 72 per cent of those who wanted out of homosexuality out of the practice.

God loves the homosexual as a person but hates the sin of homosexuality. Any casual reading of the first chapter of Romans would remove any doubt as to how God regards the sin of homosexuality. There is also no doubt that God can solve the problem of homosexuality for the 28 per cent Masters and Johnson and/or any other counselors cannot reach.

However, as I mention in another segment of the book, that person with the problem has to turn his life over to Jesus Christ, because the Lord does not change what He does not own. As my friend Bob George, a dedicated staff member at the church and formerly a very successful businessman, points out, it's very much like the radio. Today we have both AM and FM, and if you are tuned in to AM, there is absolutely no way that you can receive on FM. Of course, the opposite applies. Once the Lord owns you, and you are "tuned in" to His channel, then regardless of the sin, whether it is the sin of homosexuality, lying, stealing, drinking, adultery, or whatever, God—the Jesus that I love—can very definitely change YOU and solve the problem.

The reason Jesus Christ can solve problems which the psychiatrist cannot is very simple: man is dealing with the old nature and you simply cannot deal with the old nature and make a new man. Jesus Christ takes the old man, changes his nature, and then speaks to that new nature. As the Bible says, "When you walk in the Spirit, you will not fulfill the desires of the flesh."

HOLD THE PHONE

Now before my heterosexual friends complacently and self-righteously single out the homosexual community for scathing criticism, *and* before any homosexual who might be reading this book starts sounding off and accusing me of judging him and not knowing what I'm talking about, read on.

If I'm to believe my Bible, and I do, then the homosexual act is a sin—*period.* So is lying, cheating, stealing, swearing, adultery, vanity, pride, deceitfulness—all sin. God's Bible doesn't talk about little sins or big sins—just sin. Unfortunately, most of us (me too) have a tendency to see what other people do as big, bad, sins and our own as little, or not so bad sins. I'm not sure what language the Lord would use in responding to this feeling you and I have, but I've got an idea it comes out *baloney!*

I agree with Anita Bryant. I don't want a homosexual—either known or unknown—teaching our children in public schools, because you cannot logically suppress the emotional feeling of the individual who teaches our children. For *exactly* the same reason, I do not want a thief, prostitute, drug addict, wife-beater, child molester, egomaniac, or any other person who espouses his sin as being all right to be placed in the sensitive and responsible position of educating the *only* generation which stands between us and a satanic takeover.

DOES JESUS CHRIST MAKE A DIFFERENCE?

My friend, George Shinn, the youngest winner of the Horatio Alger Award in 1973, will emphatically state that Christ does make a difference. George was failing in the private school business on an almost unprecedented scale and was told at a meeting of his advisers there was no way he could survive. The words they used were, "George, you don't have a prayer." George left the meeting somewhat despondent, but as he was driving home it suddenly dawned on him that actually all he did have was a prayer. He pulled over to the side of the road and lifted his voice to the Living Savior who hears all prayers uttered in faith by His sons and daughters. The rest of the story is history and since the story is so beautiful, I would not repeat more than the few lines I already have. But if you want to read an inspiring story of how a shy, relatively uneducated young man turned his entire life around and helped thousands of people in the process, pick up *Good Morning, Lord* by George Shinn and you too will be inspired. I will elaborate to the extent that I share this with you. George Shinn has acquired a fortune (not the proverbial small one), an even closer relationship with his family, peace of mind, and a booming business since he took God in as his partner and then let God run the business. Yes, the *now* benefits from serving Jesus are tremendous!

A CHRISTIAN HOME IS NO GUARANTEE

When you remember someone as a well-mannered, thoughtful little boy who ran errands without complaint and who kept his room neat, it is a little difficult to picture him as a dealer in drugs, a thief, and an addict. Yet, that is what Brian Lowe, who had all the advantages of loving parents and a Christian home, turned out to be. Brian started rebelling, as far as his parents know, when he was about fifteen years old. At that time he got involved in a rock band and started doing many of the things his peer group was doing. Actually, Brian's trouble started when as a five-year-old he discovered that a little lie often meant the difference in a pat on the head or several on the rear. By thirteen he had added stealing, smoking, and vulgar language to the list, and viewed Jesus Christ in the same light as Santa Claus and the Tooth Fairy.

Like most others, Brian started on a small scale, but escalated into major problems. Petty thievery turned into breaking and entering; mischieviousness became meanness; and a first-time drunk on graduation night turned into a fifth of liquor a day. Reckless teenage driving ended up as car theft; a casual introduction to drugs led him into becoming a "speed freak" and an "acid head," unable to separate the real world from the make-believe one. He kept seeking, as he says, the big high from which you never come down. (Then, with a note of irony, he adds that several of his friends attained this goal and are now in mental institutions.) High drug usage ultimately—as it generally does—led him into dealing and the decision to become a "big-time criminal." His teacher and motivator in this decision had been the television set, where he learned everything except how to avoid getting caught. In short, Brian's problems had gotten so big they were beyond human solution.

HOW COULD IT HAPPEN?

The question is, how and why did it happen? I knew Brian as a child through working with his parents. My exposure was fairly limited, but knowing his parents as I did, it came as a complete shock when I learned he had been sentenced to eight years in prison for breaking and entering. Two weeks after Brian was sentenced, in the total emptiness of the reality of hopelessness and helplessness, God's promise in Proverbs came to pass. God tells us that if we raise our children up in the way of the Lord, when they are old they will not depart from it. In Brian's case, he had been raised in the church. As a fourteen-year-old he had been baptized. Unfortunately, his baptism was not that of conviction, but rather because his parents and his friends expected him to and he did not want to disappoint them. Unfortunately, Brian's heart was not of the Lord, but the seed of God's Word had been planted. Brian apparently did not have any religion, but God's promise that His words will not return void proved true.

NO OTHER PLACE TO GO

In the darkness of the jail cell, facing several years behind bars, in frustration and desperation Brian sought the God and the Bible of his childhood. Since preachers generally know the Bible better than others, Brian called for Dr. Paul Franklin, the pastor who had served his parents so well. Dr. Franklin responded immediately and in the quietness of Brian's cell explained the plan of salvation. Brian Lowe, on bended knees and with a broken heart, invited the Lord Jesus to come into his life.

One of the first things Dr. Franklin did was to impress upon Brian the importance of knowing God's Word. So Brian conscientiously started making time serve him by studying the Bible on a daily basis. Since Brian had a real zeal for learning God's Word, he learned a lot about what God has to say in an amazingly short period of time.

GOD CAN DO ANYTHING

It was during this period Brian wrote to me. The experience has been a tremendous inspiration to me. Soon after his incarceration Brian learned that his wife, Teresa, who has been a constant source of love and encouragement to him, was expecting their first child. The joy of the new life was clouded with the stark realization that the chances this baby would be normal were only moderate, at best. Brian had been a heavy user of amphetamines and LSD and had even established a reputation of being able to handle more LSD than anyone. Brian, as Christians arc instructed to do, turned to the God he had come to love and trust. He fervently prayed that his baby would be born normal and healthy. One of the greatest moments of the young couple's lives was the birth of Justin Whitt Lowe — a beautiful, completely normal, perfectly healthy baby boy. Equally miraculous is the fact that Brian's own mind returned to its former sharpness, which is incredible since both "speed" and LSD are notorious destroyers of brain cells. Psalm 103:1-5 explains *how* this restoration or healing came about. First Corinthians 2:16 states that we have the "mind of Christ."

Even more amazing than what God did to and for Brian's mind is what He did to Brian's heart. At the time of his sentencing Brian was filled with hatred and bitterness for everything and just about everybody, but especially toward the men who had brought him in and sentenced him to jail. Knowing the *necessity* of forgiveness and the *impossibility* of loving these men on his own, Brian prayed, "Okay, Lord, I can't love these men. It's just not in me. But You can and I will let You love them through me." In no time, Brian found himself fervently praying for them and loving them more each day. Again, again, and yet again, I will say it: "*You* can't—but *God* can!"

As Brian has corresponded with me over these months and as I have read the Scriptures he sends me, I have watched with joy and amazement his spiritual growth and faith. I have listened to his songs of praise and thanksgiving, being reminded again and again that Jesus makes a difference. Although Brian's list of offenses was long (he could have been sentenced to 160 years), he was convicted on only three counts of breaking and entering and pleaded guilty to four more. He received an eight-year sentence. It's exciting to know that after Brian was released on parole in February, 1978, after serving only about two years, society had wiped out his debt with the exception of the conditions of the parole. What's infinitely more exciting is the fact that God washed his slate clean the moment he accepted our Lord and asked for forgiveness.

THE OLD BRIAN LOWE IS DEAD

The story of Brian Lowe is just starting. Perhaps the most exciting thing is the fact that, as Brian was telling me the story, he stressed that he would have very little to say about the old— or as he put it, "dead"—Brian Lowe. He said, "You just don't talk about dead people very much unless they are extremely famous, and the Brian Lowe before Jesus Christ is now dead, so I want to talk about the new, alive, excited, grateful Brian Lowe."

One of the more exciting parts of his story is the way he abandoned the tobacco habit. When Brian accepted Christ and invited Him to come into his heart, that meant that Christ was "in his body," which simply means that if Brian Lowe was smoking, he was forcing smoke upon our Lord. He was a three-pack-a-day smoker who had tried desperately without success to quit. Finally, one day in complete frustration and exasperation, he threw up his hands in surrender and said, "Lord, it's obvious I cannot quit smoking, so if You want me to quit, You've got to do it, and Lord, You really need to do it in a hurry! I'm going to quit trying to quit smoking; I'm just going to smoke any time I have the urge. So Lord, I turn this problem completely over to You, and I'm going to just get out of the way." The next morning Brian smoked a pipe of tobacco as he was reading his Bible. Again that evening he smoked, but he realized that he had not smoked during the day. From that day until this, Brian Lowe has been free of the smoking habit.

The message is so beautiful—so simple, and so clear—we can't, but God can. That's the kind of Lord we have. The Lord's power is obviously not confined to breaking the smoking habit. He's in the restoration business. He restores lost souls and He does whatever needs to be done to restore those souls. He can break the habit of sin, whatever that habit or sin might be. Our responsibility, and opportunity, is to "take it to the Lord in prayer." His promise (now remember, He's the God who *cannot* lie) is to solve the problem.

THE BRIAN LOWE GOD INTENDED HIM TO BE

As I write these words, Brian Lowe is in the process of being released from the State Correctional Institute at Staunton, Virginia. He's been called to preach and is studying daily in preparation for this high calling. Correspondence from Brian's parents today is full of love, hope, and gratitude to an all-loving Heavenly Father. On the way to this condition they went through an enormous amount of grief. They shed rivers of tears through many sleepless nights. Their hearts were heavy and they lived in fear for Brian's life, his physical and mental well-being, and for his soul. Today his mother expresses it: "My heart is full of love and praise to a loving Father who loves and forgives us when we fail Him in so many ways. I thank God every day for giving us strength, love, and friends to help us through the bad times. We're especially grateful, as members of the Lampligh-ters (a gospel quartet), for the privilege of singing the Good News of Jesus. The constant reminders as we 'hailed the power of Jesus's name' gave us peace as we were 'standing on the promises of God.' "

As Whitt and Wanda Lowe express it, "When Brian was saved and called into the ministry, we knew then it was worth it all." They stated that when Brian came home on a weekend furlough and was baptized and spoke in their church they knew, in a very small way, the joy our Heavenly Father feels when a rebellious child comes back to Him. It's much like what happens when an old, ugly caterpillar breaks forth from the cocoon and spreads forth its wings to become the beautiful creature it was intended to be. They felt in church that day they were seeing the beginning of the man God intended Brian to be.

That's the glorious thing about our Lord. If we will permit Him to, Jesus will continue to love and build us into what He wants us to be. The best part of the Brian Lowe story is yet to come because he is a spiritual "baby" in the Lord. Fortunately, he's feeding on the "meat" of the Scriptures, so as he grows into manhood I know God will continue to use him in more and more ways. As Bill Gothard says, Brian is on God's easel, and God is busily working on him to make him the completed man he was meant to be.

GREATER LOVE HATH NO MAN

Several years ago I heard this story but its real impact hit me as I was writing this book and after I understood what "love" is all about. A young businessman on his way home from work was seriously injured in a traffic accident and lost a lot of blood. His life hung in the balance and a blood transfusion was desperately needed. However, he had a rare type of blood and a donor could not be found. Finally, someone suggested that his nine-year-old daughter Kathy might have the same type. Kathy's mother asked her if she would be willing to give her daddy some of her blood so that he might live. Kathy bit her lip, paused for a second, and then agreed to do it.

Her blood was the same type, the transfusion was made, and the crisis passed. Little Kathy lay on the table after the transfusion, her body almost as white as the sheets she lay on. After a few minutes her mother came into the room and told her that the doctor said it was all right for her to get up and go home. Kathy looked at her mother in shocked disbelief and said, "Mother, you mean I'm not going to die?" It's obvious that little Kathy thought she was laying down her life so that her father could live. Don't you know the young businessman was overcome with the love he felt for a daughter whom he undoubtedly already loved very dearly. Can you imagine a love so great? I'll have to confess that at one time I could not imagine such a love. Then I met Jesus—and love. When He gave up His heavenly throne to come to earth He *knew* what was involved. He *knew* that He would go to Calvary. He knew what the agony of the cross would be. He *knew* He would suffer and bleed and die, but He loved you and me so much that He willingly gave up His own life so that whosoever *believeth* in Him should not perish but have everlasting life. Surely you want to live forever and you can, just by believing. Do you believe? If not, have you asked God to give you belief?

JESUS UNDERSTANDS PORTUGESE, SPANISH, ETC.

As you have probably noticed, I keep saying in a lot of different ways that I love the Lord for many reasons and that exciting things are always happening when you are in fellowship with Him. One day in our Sunday school class, which often turns into a miniature revival, we had a missionary who spoke only Portuguese. He would speak and our interpreter would translate what he was saying. After class, Jack Glasscock, a friend and member of the class, commented, "You know, Zig, that was a beautiful experience. But for one of God's most meaningful experiences, you should hear someone pray in a foreign language." Then it dawned loud and clear—our Lord and Savior understands all languages. There are no communication barriers between us and Him.

About three Sundays later at the end of our service, when our pastor opened the doors of the church for membership for those who acknowledge Jesus Christ as Lord and Savior, a deaf mute came forth. We have a "Silent Friends" portion of our service, and through sign language a little girl came to know the love of Jesus Christ. When she stepped forward to publicly acknowledge Jesus as Lord and Savior, there were few dry eyes in the church. The realization that you don't even have to have the capacity to speak in order for our Lord to know your heart and extend eternity to you was too much for those of us who know Him.

As I was working on the manuscript for this book still another beautiful incident took place. When the doors of the church were opened for membership and rededication, a blind girl came forth and gave her life completely to the Lord. The Bible clearly says that man judges from outer appearances—with the eyes—but God looks into the heart. When the blind girl came forth it hit me again why we must not judge others. We use our eyes and look on the outer surface of man because that's all eyes can do. We know that's not enough because there are millions of sighted people who have been exposed to Jesus Christ but who haven't "seen" Him yet. How much better to be like the blind girl and be able to see with the heart! She clearly sees Him, and after a brief sightless journey on the planet earth (to God a thousand years is as a day [II Peter 3:8]), she will have a panoramic view of God's universe forever.

ADMIT ANYONE—WHO KNOWS JESUS

One Sunday a man in this thirties but with the mind of a child came down to give his life to the Lord. I'm certain he will never understand many of the theological discussions which take place in many of the sanctuaries, but isn't it wonderful to know that this man-child knows *everything* he needs to know to spend eternity with our Lord? He knows Jesus loves him, that He died for him, that He arose triumphant from the grave. He knows and he believes, which puts him light-years ahead of some of the theological morticians who are educated beyond their intelligence. They are the ones who often miss out on the saving grace of our Savior who said, "Suffer little children, and forbid them not, to come unto me: for of such is the kingdom of heaven" (Matthew 19:14). I've seen them come from every race, creed, and color, the mighty and the humble, the old and the young, the rich and the poor. It's exciting to know that even though some of the high and the mighty can get in to see some of the more important people (all people are important to God) here on planet earth, *all* of us will be admitted to the presence of God, without standing in line, through our belief in and the grace of Jesus Christ.

After I dedicated my life to the Lord, I had a unique and exciting experience on my first visit back to my mother's home in Yazoo City, Mississippi. I sat by her bed and read my Bible to her. By that time my mother's mind was largely gone. I had no way of knowing whether or not she understood anything I was saying. The next day, however, she told my sister and her husband that her son had been home and that he had preached to her. (She even said I was a good preacher, but then what would you expect a mother to say about her son?) I knew then that God had cleared her mind for the occasion so she could know that all her years of praying for me and witnessing to me had not been in vain.

The Lord used my mother's illness to bring my younger brother back into the fold to a new understanding and acceptance of Jesus Christ. He was extremely close to my mother, loved her as much as any son can love his mother, and respected her for all the things she represented. The Lord moved me to explain to him that as good as our mother was, she was not good enough to spend eternity with Christ. No human being was good enough, and if he thought Mother or anyone else would ever get to heaven on goodness he was sadly mistaken. At first it was difficult for him to understand that the mother whom he loved so deeply was not good enough to be with Jesus and that she would be in heaven only because salvation is a gift, free and clear. I explained to him that anybody could have salvation by believing, and *only* by believing, and therefore he need never worry or fret as to whether or not he was good enough to spend eternity with the Lord. He certainly wasn't. Once my brother, Judge Ziglar, understood that nobody was good enough, that everyone gets there through grace and belief in Jesus Christ, the whole picture was clear. He then invited the Lord Jesus to come into his life, also.

One of my most exciting experiences has been to watch him grow in the Lord and to lead the lost members of his family to Christ. The changes in him have truly been dramatic. He, too, is enjoying the now benefits of peace, joy, happiness, love, and excitement. His physical and financial health have dramatically improved and his speaking career has catapulted upward.

On another occasion we were together for a family reunion which was held primarily because of Mother's illness. On this occasion brother Huie, who has so much love and compassion, was used by God to lead Julie, our youngest daughter, to Christ. Her faith is truly a beautiful sight to witness. Her mother and I marvel at it and praise God for His goodness in giving us such a blessing. What a thrill it must be to my mother to know that God used her illness to claim a son and a granddaughter for His Kingdom!

THE SMORGASBORD LINE IS STILL OPEN

In Psalm 34:10 we learn, "They that seek the Lord shall not want *any* good thing." Now, "shall not want any good thing" covers a lot of territory. As a happy Christian I get excited about promises like that because I, like many other people, enjoy good things. Knowing that His children can misunderstand Him, God repeats Himself many times. In Psalm 37:4 He says, "Delight thyself also in the Lord and He shall give thee the desires of thine heart." A promise like that from a person would be impossible, but that promise from the God who cannot lie is exciting.

REMEMBER: The more you thank God for what you have, the more you will have to thank God for.

First "Thank You" Date _____

Second "Thank You" Date _____

THANK YOU, LORD

FOR:

1. _____

2. _____

3. _____

4. _____

5. _____

6. _____

7. _____

8. _____

9. _____

10. _____

11. _____

12. _____

You can win every game you play, but if you don't know Jesus as Lord, you are the biggest loser of all.
—GRANT TEAFF, Baylor University, Coach of the Year, 1974

YOU CAN'T KNOW LOVE
UNTIL YOU KNOW THE GIVER OF LOVE.

The man or woman who is wholly and joyously surrendered to Christ cannot make a wrong choice. Any choice will be the right one. — Dr. A. W. Tozer

---

If you don't know God's love it is because you don't love God.

Learn to serve and you learn to love.

If you know only the stern judgment of God it is easy to sin — when you know the infinite love of God it is difficult to sin.

Many times Christians state their love for the Lord and their willingness to die for Him. I will make no pretense of knowing the Lord's will in your life, but I do feel that in most cases the Lord is far more interested in our living for Him than He is in our dying for Him.

CHAPTER EIGHT

But Lord I've Got a Car Payment and It's Due Next Thursday

BREAD BEFORE FORGIVENESS OF SINS

There is nothing you will ever face that you and God can't handle. The Lord promises us He will give us the grace to bear whatever burden comes our way. But, unfortunately, many people have complete faith in the incredible and very little faith in the simple day-to-day promises our Lord makes. Many Christians have no trouble with, "In the beginning God created the Heavens and the Earth." Or, "Go thy way: thy faith hath made thee whole" (Mark 10:52). They have no trouble believing He parted the waters of the Red Sea so that approximately three million Jews could walk through. They have no trouble believing that Christ walked on water, arose from the dead, or fed the multitudes. They have no trouble believing the big things, but "You see, Lord, I've got this car payment, it's due next Thursday, and it is nearly two hundred dollars. Let's face it, Lord, You might can split water, but you've never dealt with a finance company before."

Amazing! It never occurs to many "believers" that the same God who created the universe can figure out a way to resolve the differences between husband and wife. Surely the Jesus who stilled the winds and arose triumphant over death can solve the problems of drink or bring parent and child into a loving communicating relationship. Just as surely, the same Jesus who was subjected to *all* the temptations you and I are subject to, yet lived without sin, can fulfill His promise that He will not *permit* us to be tempted beyond that which we can bear. As a believer, surely it makes sense that the God who parted the Red Sea and hung the earth from nothing (Job 26:7) can give you the solution to your current problem and even make it possible to handle that car or house payment. Surely it makes sense that the Lord who knew how to create the world knows how to run it—including even your life.

Personally, I believe that the same Jesus who knows and cares when a single sparrow falls, and is so concerned about our *daily* needs that He taught us to pray in the Lord's Prayer for our daily bread even *before* we ask for forgiveness, will intercede in all areas of our life *if* we ask Him to and believe He will. Yes, the Savior I love and worship is an everyday, every need Lord who knows my needs and supplies them even *before* I ask (Matthew 6:8).

FAITH IS A FOOTBALL GAME

In this sophisticated world of the 1970s there are many people who say they do not have faith in the things they cannot see. Then they take a deep breath of air, which seems a little inconsistent. Personally, I would have no faith in air I *could* see! Many people say they do not have faith in things they do not understand, which is pretty ridiculous because most of us do not understand much of what goes on around us every day. We flip a light switch in faith. Most of us don't understand how the flowing of water in a faraway river is translated into light in our living room, but we get as much light from the bulb as the most brilliant electrical engineer. It's in faith that we flip the switch to light a room. A savage from the depths of the jungle would be astonished if he were suddenly dropped into a darkened living room and observed what happens when the light switch is turned on. What's even more astonishing to me is the realization that we have the power and light of the entire universe at our disposal just by turning our lives, in faith, over to Jesus Christ.

We pull into a service station in a strange town a thousand miles from home and, despite the fact that our mobility is entirely dependent upon gasoline rather than buttermilk being in that pump, we invite a complete stranger to "fill it up." We do it in faith. We give our small baby milk from a carton bought in an out-of-the-way store from people we don't know. The store got that milk from a delivery man they seldom see. The milk company bought it from a dairy they had never visited and from cows they don't even know. Yes, faith in our fellow man is necessary, isn't it?

THE "HAIL MARY"

My idea of faith, however, is best explained in a football game I saw. This game was between the Dallas Cowboys and the Minnesota Vikings, and I shall report it factually and without bias. I'll just report it as any dedicated, committed, dyed-in-the-wool, loyal Dallas Cowboy fan would report a game. It was the 1975 playoff game. Although it was obvious to every Cowboy fan that ours was the best team, we headed into the final minute with the Vikings ahead. Many of the Cowboy faithful had lost their faith. There was weeping and wailing and gnashing of teeth. They were saying things like, "Same old Cowboys. We don't get beat—we beat ourselves. Should've won the game, just blew it, that's all." However, as I sat watching the game, I'm going to tell you there was not the slightest doubt in my mind as to the outcome of the game. My confidence in the Cowboys was total. I assured those who were with me they should not worry about a thing, that everything was under control, that we would pull this one out for sure. We were on our own twenty-six yard line and faced a fourth down with nineteen yards needed for a first down. Roger Staubach, the Dallas quarterback, got into the shotgun formation and hit Drew Pearson going down the right sideline for twenty-five yards. The stands went wild, but to be honest, I kept my seat and refrained from any such emotional outburst. Why should I get carried away about a football game which I was totally confident was ours? Next play, Staubach missed on a pass and the crowd groaned. Thirty-six seconds remained. The Cowboys faced a second down with ten yards to go for a first down, but my faith was still complete; there was absolutely no doubt in my mind about the outcome of the game.

WHY SHOULD I WORRY?

Then, as all you football fans remember, there was the biggie—Staubach faded back and Drew Pearson took off for the end zone, forty-nine yards away. The quarterback let go with what many people have referred to as his "Hail Mary." However, the television cameras focusing on Staubach's face just before he set this particular play in motion revealed the face of a man who also had confidence which goes beyond just being confident. There was the trace of a smile on his face, as if to say, "Don't worry about a thing." I didn't. That pass stayed up in the air for two minutes and twenty-eight seconds. (All right, maybe it wasn't *quite* that long!) Pearson was headed straight for the end zone when he was surrounded by two of the Minnesota Vikings. Despite their best efforts, Pearson calmly caught the ball, hugged it to his hip, and stepped unmolested into the end zone with the winning score. The crowd literally exploded. I believe had there been a roof on the stadium it would have come off. However, I can again say to you in total honesty that I kept my seat and simply smiled broadly at what had just happened. I stress to you again that not once did my faith ever waver. Not once was there any doubt in my mind about the ultimate outcome of the game. I knew, and I *knew* that I knew, that the Cowboys would come out on top.

Now, in all honesty I must confess to you that one of the reasons for my total confidence was the fact that I was watching a replay of the game. Rather obviously, you as a reader will feel that the story up until this point is pretty silly. After all, Zig, you are probably saying, you knew the final score—you *knew* the Cowboys had won, so why should you either worry or get excited? This, of course, is my point. You see, the game of football is played by certain rules and if you break enough of the rules— regardless of how good you are—you're going to lose the game.

THE OTHER GAME—THE ONE CALLED LIFE

Now there is another game—it's called *life*. It's a bigger game, lasts longer, involves considerably more, and is a great deal more important. There is also a book of rules for this game of life. It's called the Holy Bible. To be completely honest, I have read this Book, and to be candid, I cheated just a little since I read the last page. I know exactly how the game is going to end and I *know* I have won that game. I know the decision is irreversible and irrevocable. Here's my question: if I know how the game is going to end and I know I've won, then why should I get upset when I'm penalized for some rule infraction, even though the penalty was unwarranted? Knowing what I know about the way the game ends enables me "not to sweat the small stuff," even if an official blows a call or I am unjustly penalized or unfairly treated. I might not like everything that happens along the way, but I still have the total assurance that I'm the winner of the game called life. I win not because of my own efforts or my own goodness, but rather through the grace, love, and mercy of my Lord and Savior, Jesus Christ. He died so that I might win this game of life and live with Him forever.

I was not nervous about the football game because I already knew the final score. I say the same thing about salvation. I'm not the least bit nervous about the outcome because God has already told me the final score, and it's a total victory. Not only that, but God, through His rule book and score card, the Holy Bible, assures me that as of this moment I'm ahead in the game. He cautions me to pray constantly (I Thessalonians 5:17) and to surround myself with His Word and salvation's full armor. He even tells me that when I'm temporarily thrown for a loss that I'm not to worry because "If God be for us, who can be against us?" (Romans 8:31). The ultimate victory is eternity with Jesus Christ and it is irrevocably guaranteed. Paul tells us in Romans 8:38, "For I am persuaded that neither death nor life nor angels nor principalities nor powers nor things present nor things to come nor height nor depth nor any other creature shall be able to separate us from the love of God which is in Christ Jesus our Lord." As far as I can see, that covers it all, and if we're not separated from the love of Jesus Christ then He who has the power to save us not only will save us but will keep us forever secure.

My question to you is simple and my point is contained in the question: if you know how all of the tomorrows of your life are going to end, and you know that you've won them all, doesn't it make sense that you can deal more effectively with today?

I CONFESS

The answer to that question has got to be a rather obvious "yes." That's the reason I wrote *Confessions of A Happy Christian*, because there are so many people who view Christianity as the "give-up" religion. They think entirely in terms of what you have to "give up" if you accept Christ as Lord. They think in these terms: you've got to give up drinking, give up smoking, give up fishing and hunting and golf and sleeping late on Sunday morning, give up telling dirty stories, using profanity, being caustic and critical of other people, give up laughing and all worldly ambitions, and a thousand and one other things which many people have labeled as "fun" and "happiness." It's astonishing how effective Satan has been in selling the idea that in order to have fun you've got to sin in the process.

Since this book is a confession, I guess that I'll have to confess and say that for years I was part of the crowd. I did not want to give up a lot of these things. Interestingly enough, I especially hated to give up some of the little jokes I was telling from the platform. Now they were not *real* bad. They were simply questionable, and besides, people seemed to enjoy them. At least they laughed at them. The rest of my confession, though, is the exciting part. I confess to you that when I gave up the occasional cocktail and the slightly off-color story, that it wasn't a give-up. It was an exchange. I exchanged those drinks and stories for a considerably clearer mind and definitely a cleaner one than the one I'd previously had. What are the results? In a word—*spectacular*! My own peace of mind far surpasses what I had before. Interestingly enough, I now get many more compliments and much more laughter in my sessions than I did before. As a matter of fact, another confession I'll make is this: I was listening to one of my cassette recordings the day before I wrote these words and realized that just seven years ago we were having to add canned laughter to my recordings because the audiences were not laughing loudly enough at my humor. Today that is no longer necessary.

I BELIEVE JESUS HAS A SENSE OF HUMOR

Those who know me are aware of the fact that I'm inclined to tell a few stories along the way. I think humor is one of the great gifts of life and I believe our Lord is happy with any humor that glorifies both God and man. When I made my commitment to the Lord I also knew that I would not—could not—tell a joke or story that would not be appropriate to repeat in front of my Lord on Judgment Day. God has taken this commitment and used it in a wonderful way. Don't misunderstand. I never did tell really dirty, off-color stories to my audiences. Satan used me more effectively and cleverly than that. Since people have a tendency to see what they want to see and hear what they want to hear, I really created a lot of confusion, which is Satan's specialty. In addition to my slightly off-color stories, I also would generally make some scriptural references, and that really created confusion! The good guys thought I was one of them, and the bad guys thought I was one of them. Satan *knew* I was his and he used me quite effectively.

Then Jesus Christ came in and the questionable stories went out. The results have been exciting. Audiences respond much more positively to good, clean stories (of course, today I've got a much better writer!). Some people think God has no sense of humor but, my friend, if you will just read your Bible you will find this just isn't so. Remember the story of Abraham and Sarah? When God's angel told the ninety-nine-year-old Abraham that he was going to father a child and be the head of a great nation, Abraham literally got down on the ground and rolled around laughing (Genesis 17:17). Sarah laughed too, but since she would be more involved, she didn't get down on the ground to do her laughing.

SOMETHING ELSE TO "GIVE UP"

As a Christian, I have noticed a lot of things happening in my life since that eventful July 4, 1972. There is a difference in my presentation. I say this gratefully and not boastfully because I clearly understand John 15:5, 6 and 7. People tell me that there is a new dimension, an added depth, an obvious power that was lacking earlier. I accept this as valid because my calendar is much busier now than it was when I was handling my life on my own. I no longer accept engagements that will take me out of God's house on Sunday, and I no longer work on Sunday. The one time that I made an exception to that, the Lord taught me a vital lesson. I had worked all Sunday afternoon and evening, preparing two proposals and doing some writing which I rationalized had to be done because the "ox was in the ditch." I just knew that I was going to make two big sales. The work I did was, I thought, excellent. I got the proposals in the mail to the companies and received a resounding "no" from each of them. I am a faster learner now than I used to be, so another one of those things I gave up was working on Sunday.

As a born-again Christian *I* did not really give up anything. For the first time in my life I now do everything I want to. Now, I'll be the first to admit that my "want-to's" have undergone some dramatic changes, because the old me no longer exists. I am a new creature (II Corinthians 5:17), and the old things that formerly pleased me are now repulsive to me.

SPIRITUAL GROWTH

Many times we see people turn their lives over to the Lord with great enthusiasm. They are in the church every time the doors open; they profess their faith; they study their Bibles. However, over a period of years, much of this initial enthusiasm dies. I personally believe this little story explains the reason this can and does happen.

In Israel there are two seas fed by the River Jordan. One is the Sea of Galilee and the other one is the Dead Sea. Today on the shores of the Sea of Galilee you see children at play, fishermen at work, and commerce busily functioning. The Sea of Galilee is fed by the River Jordan. As a matter of fact, the River

Jordan runs in one end of the Sea and out the other. For every drop of water the Sea of Galilee accepts at one end from the River Jordan it gives back another drop to the River Jordan from the other end. Further downstream the Jordan River ends as it runs into the Dead Sea. The Dead Sea is as dead as its name. There is no life in that sea. Activity is largely confined to tourists who come to see the phenomenon for a short visit. Nobody stays very long. The Dead Sea is a hoarder. It takes a lot of water from the Jordan River, but it does not return any of what it takes to any other body. The result is stagnation and death.

Unfortunately, this is often the way Christians perform. They accept the teachings of others; they read the Bible; they even pray. Initially their intentions are good. Their excitement is great. But if they only *take in* the Good News, their Christian life and effectiveness are extremely limited. This is the law God laid down thousands of years ago. As you sow, so also shall you reap. These Christian brothers and sisters who are sowing little will reap little. I believe the greatest opportunity and responsibility we as Christians have is to share the Word and share our faith. It is the *only* way we have to lead someone else to the Lord. Additionally, it has long been an established educational fact that a good teacher will learn more than a good student. The best way for our faith to grow and expand is by expressing that faith to others.

Unfortunately, many Christians plead ignorance of the Bible and maintain they do not know enough to teach a Sunday school class. Additionally, they get such a "blessing" from sitting in someone else's class. It's definitely true that your heart should be right, and you need to feel led to teach a class or share the Word. However, you do not have to be a theologian or a Bible scholar to share your faith and teach a class of small children. If we wait until we know everything before we start sharing, we will never share because no one knows all the mysteries of God. By the same token, if you "wait until all the lights are green before you leave for town," you will stay at home the rest of your life. Each of us must start from where we are with what we have and go from there. Then God will take the knowledge we have, expand it, and use our witness to claim others for Himself.

Personally, I am convinced that the person who truly loves the Lord is far more effective as a witness and a teacher than one who is theologically well informed but who doesn't have a personal relationship with Jesus. It has been accurately stated that "people don't care how much you know—until they know how much you care." From where I sit, I'm convinced that the lost person will respond to a sincere believer far better than to an insincere Bible scholar. However, let me urge you not to get smug in your sincere ignorance, because if you are truly sincere you will immediately start searching for God's truths to go with your belief. When you search, Jesus gives you this promise: "I thank Thee, O Father, Lord of Heaven and Earth, that Thou hast hid these things from the wise and prudent and hast revealed them unto babes." So it is very clear that God will reveal His Word to us. It is amazing how much God can do with one dedicated life in a short period of time, as the story of Les Mills so beautifully proves.

On October 25, 1977, I was in the Hyatt House in Birmingham, Alabama, having dinner when I bumped into my old friend Bobby Wisinger, who is the regional manager for the Kirby Vacuum Cleaner Company. Bobby is an enthusiastic, dedicated man who is a business and a personal success because he knows the Lord, so I was doubly glad to see him. While we were visiting over dinner he mentioned Les Mills and asked if I knew that Les had recently died. I told him that I had not heard and asked for details. Then Bobby said, "Well, there are a lot of people who loved and miss Les Mills. His story is truly an inspiration to many, many people." He shared some of the circumstances and urged me to call Evelyn and get the details. This is the story of Les Mills which Evelyn shared with me.

A ROLLER COASTER LIFE

Les and Evelyn Mills married at the ripe old age of seventeen and lived twenty years together on planet earth before Les was called home. Les was a salesman who did everything from running a bread route and paper route to selling insurance and briefly working as a waiter before settling down to a career with the Kirby Company. They had a tough start and had it not been for the helping hand of an immigrant from Thailand named Danny Voravudhi, who helped him get his first car, things would have been even more difficult for Les and Evelyn. The car was a 1953 Chevrolet with the floorboard missing on the driver's side. Les stuffed it with an old army blanket and proceeded to freeze on his way to his demonstrations. Net results: he decided to leave the winters of Bethesda, Maryland, and go back home to North Carolina.

While in Whiteville, North Carolina, Les and Evelyn were faithful in their church attendance. Les came close to a commitment to the Lord and Evelyn put her trust in the Lord. However, as it often happens, there are those whose conduct leaves serious questions as to their sincerity, and this often negatively affects the lives of many others whose faith has not matured. In Evelyn and Les's case, a young minister was making weekly trips from Fayetteville, North Carolina, to Whiteville to conduct the services. He was about Les's age, and Les developed a closeness to him. The young man had a family, including a small baby, and wanted to move to Whiteville so that he could be of service as a minister, counseling and visiting the sick. However, when he made this proposal, and Evelyn is convinced it was made out of the depth of his love, the church with one week's notice simply cut him off. Les felt this was hypocritical and withdrew from the church and, as Evelyn said, she herself did some backsliding.

Les had an up-and-down, roller coaster-type career for a number of years, and was inclined to drink, gamble, and on occasion get a little loud and rambunctious. Again, his friend Danny Voravudhi came to the rescue and persuaded him to move to Florence, South Carolina, and work with him. A year later he moved to Columbia, South Carolina, and then in December of 1971 Les and Evelyn moved to Greenville, South Carolina. In June of 1973, after winning a national contest, Les and Evelyn went to Andrews, Texas, to see the new factory which had just been opened. Upon arrival they had a call from Les's sister who said their fifteen-year-old son Buddy (Leslie E. Mills III) had disappeared with the car and his girlfriend. Someone asked Les what he was going to do about it. Les simply responded, "I'm going to try to get my boy back. All he's doing is following the example his dad has set for him." Evelyn and Les spent the most miserable night of their lives flying all night to get back home. They were drawn closer to God and, as it often happens, closer together as they prayed every step of the way. They located their son in New Bern, North Carolina, and persuaded him to return home.

Although this experience was a sobering one in many ways, it was not until much later that the commitment was made. Again, the Lord used a difficult circumstance to show His love. It was at a V.I.P. Convention and, as Evelyn pointed out, the family, including Buddy and his wife, as well as some friends of theirs, were drinking together. Les and Buddy got into a violent argument. Buddy, under the influence of alcohol, told Les he hated him. This happened despite the fact they had always been extremely close, were golfing buddies, and had deep affection for each other. After a sleepless night, Les called Buddy at his hotel room and they got together for a talk. Les promised Buddy that he never again would take a drink and asked Buddy to make the same commitment. This was a big step in the right direction to heal the wound between father and son, but it wasn't the final step that was to bring Les to that walk with *his* Father in heaven.

BUILDING ON THE ROCK OF LOVE

The final step came when the Edgewood Baptist Church in Greenville, South Carolina, called Evelyn and said they wanted to buy a Kirby. She went over, demonstrated the Kirby, felt the warmth and friendliness of the people, and persuaded Les to visit the church. Les and Evelyn had been taking the children to another church, but they had not been attending because they did not feel any warmth or love from the members. At Edgewood they fell in love with the people, the pastor, and the environment. It was here that Les Mills committed his life totally and without reservation to Jesus Christ.

Six weeks later, while at another meeting in Nashville, Tennessee, Les felt a lump near the back of his neck. The doctor thought it was a swollen gland, gave him some medication, and told him if it persisted to come back. Two weeks later the lump was larger, so the doctor performed a biopsy and discovered it was malignant. The operation was apparently successful, although they were cautioned that the surgeons might not have gotten the source. The operation was followed by twenty-nine cobalt treatments in seven weeks, during which Les dropped from a robust 212 pounds to 156 pounds. Three weeks after the treatments stopped another lump appeared. What followed would have been, for the non-Christian, an intolerable, unbearable situation: five more operations in Buffalo, New York, and many trips with Evelyn to Philadelphia, Pennsylvania, for additional treatment. He was often there from one to three weeks and would frequently return to Greenville, only to have to turn around and go back to Philadelphia.

During this period Les and Evelyn, when they were in Greenville, attended church every time the doors opened. Many times Les told Evelyn that the happiest period of his life was the fifteen months after he accepted the Lord as Savior until he went to be with Him. Although the pain he suffered was excruciating, not once did he utter a complaint, not once did he ever say he was hurting. The result is that Jesus Christ used the life and story of Les and Evelyn Mills in a truly beautiful way. Les was so obviously committed to the Lord that he was made a deacon at the church in just six months. This in itself is almost unheard of, but as I indicated in an earlier chapter, when you have sold out lock, stock, and barrel to Jesus Christ, there is a difference in you. Other Christians can easily see the change in spirit. Not only was Les made a deacon in such a short length of time, but he was elevated to that position without being asked a single question. Les's pastor Joseph D. Seay said this was something he had never before seen happen. His fellow deacons and other church members knew Les was a man walking with his hand firmly in the hand of our Lord.

When Les Mills made his commitment it was an all-out one. The church membership grew by a significant number as a direct result of Les, his enthusiasm, and his love for the Lord. He was so interested in serving he told Evelyn if he recovered from the cancer he was going to devote all of his time to serving the Lord and let her run the business. Evelyn had—and has—a great ability to run a business,, and the Lord has blessed them financially beyond their wildest dreams. Les was especially interested in athletics and wanted to establish a recreational program for the church. Les is now watching from a Heavenly grandstand while the members are thoroughly enjoying the Les Mills Memorial Athletic Field and praising God while building their bodies.

I SHOULD BE CRYING FOR YOU

The story of Les Mills is beautiful, but by far the most beautiful and significant part of the story is what happened in the last twenty-four hours of his life. Les was pronounced clinically dead on March 24, 1977, and the members of the family were taken to another room so they might begin preparing his body for burial. Shortly thereafter a nurse walked into the room, detected signs of life, and called the doctor. Twenty minutes after the doctor had pronounced him clinically dead, Bobby Wisinger walked down the hall to tell Evelyn that Les still lived and had made a miraculous recovery.

That evening, Les Mills sat on the side of his bed talking to several of his friends, fellow distributors, and his pastor. He talked to each person, telling them individually of his commitment to the Lord and challenging each to do exactly the same thing. He told each one Jesus Christ was the *only* way, that serving Him was the most beautiful life a person could live, that he'd had more happiness in fifteen months than he'd had in the preceding thirty-six years of his life. The impact was understandably great, and at least one of these men has made a total commitment of his life. The others have been drawn closer to Christ. That evening, in talking with Evelyn, Les said to her, "I don't want you crying for me. I know I'm going to be with the Lord and as you could see, heaven is a beautiful place." As a matter of fact, he said to Evelyn, "I should be crying for you instead of you crying for me!" Then he described the yellow ribbons and the beautiful flowers he had seen. He was a little puzzled that Evelyn did not remember seeing the things he had seen since they had been together. Evelyn and the pastor feel as I do, that Les had taken those first few steps through eternity with Jesus Christ, that he had gotten a glimpse of the other side. They feel Les knew where he was going was more beautiful than what he was leaving.

The next morning, March 25, the body of Leslie E. Mills II ceased to function on planet earth, and he started that eternal walk with our Lord. Among his last words was the promise to Evelyn that they would be back together again in a matter of moments as God's calendar runs. He asked her to do what she had long ago decided to do—to continue to live for and walk with Jesus Christ.

It is my privilege to share the love of our Lord with a lot of people and have others share their love of the Lord with me. I must confess to you that as I heard the story of Les Mills and as I attempt to communicate the story to you, my heart is overflowing. How marvelous to know a Savior who can totally change a man who for nearly thirty-six years was up and down, a man who lived a life outside the Lord's will most of the time. To take that changed man and in just fifteen short months turn him into a man of love, dedication, and service so members of the family and church as well as hundreds—perhaps thousands—of others around the country will be touched by that new man—what an inspiring life!

Of all the stories of faith I've been permitted to share I am hard pressed to think of one as beautiful as the story of Les Mills. As I write, my heart is filled with love and the hope that if you do not know the Lord this story will be used by Him to bring you closer to Jesus and to His Kingdom. I might point out that if, at this moment, you have more of an awareness of the awesome love and the power of that love through Jesus Christ, you are even now the partaker of God's heavenly smorgasbord served here on planet earth.

REMEMBER: The more you thank God for what you have, the more you will have to thank God for.

First "Thank You" Date _____

Second "Thank You" Date _____

THANK YOU, LORD
FOR:

1. _____
2. _____
3. _____
4. _____
5. _____
6. _____
7. _____
8. _____
9. _____
10. _____
11. _____
12. _____

It is better to have a heart without words
than to have words without a heart.

PROF. LUIS PANTOJA

CHAPTER NINE

You'd Better Not "Witness"

When I first turned my life over to the Lord some of my friends and associates cautioned me—"for my own good"—not to try to convert the world. They suggested I had a good thing going and that I would upset others and offend a lot of people if I mentioned Jesus Christ in my talks. Interesting, isn't it? One man can tell a dirty joke and use profanity, often without censure, and another is urged not to talk about Jesus Christ.

As I go around the country speaking to various groups I have an opportunity to witness daily to large groups of people. I never cease to be amazed at the people who express admiration for my courage in witnessing publicly. I say this because personally I feel that I have a degree of courage but not enough *not* to witness. I shall never forget one program chairman who had asked me to speak along with three other speakers. Just before I was scheduled to be introduced, he told me that the audience had come to hear me speak on sales training and didn't want to hear my views on religion. He pointed out that the audience was mixed and had some Jews, some atheists, Hindus, etc. present, and he didn't want to "offend" anyone.

I responded that I knew what he was saying, but asked if it would be all right if I told a few dirty jokes. Somewhat shocked, he told me he thought a man should use good judgment in what he did. Then I pointed out that my Christian brothers and I were offended by profanity and off-color stories and asked if he had cautioned the other three speakers not to offend us. He told me he had urged them to use "good judgment," so I promised him I, too, would use good judgment—and I did. It was exciting and funny. When I got my "commercial" in for the Lord, I was interrupted with a round of applause. At that point it was all I could do to refrain from turning to the chairman and saying, "You see, Friend, the world is hungry for the Good News and—given a choice—they prefer to hear a speaker mention a perfect Savior than to tell a dirty joke laced with profanity!"

SPEAK UP, CHRISTIAN

During the last five years I have come to feel when people tell you not to witness or to let your life and not your mouth be your witness that some, maybe all of it, is either Satan or fear (which is the same thing) inspired. Satan's victory comes when he can close the mouth of the committed Christian. Just because a person sees that you are honest, thoughtful, loyal, enthusiastic, considerate, and optimistic doesn't mean that the viewer will know *why* you have such an outlook on life. I know many people who profess no faith of any kind who have these qualities in larger quantities than some professing Christians. I often meet many members of the various cults who, if they believe what they say they believe, do not really know Jesus. Yet they have many excellent qualities. To be good in the eyes of the world is one thing. To be *saved* is another matter. I feel very strongly that as a Christian I'm supposed to live a victorious Christian life ("let your light so shine," Matt. 5:16). And I'm supposed to tell others—when the occasion permits—why and how I can, through Jesus Christ, live the way I do. Incidentally, that's not a "feeling"; those are direct orders from my Heavenly Father ("Go ye into all the world, and preach the gospel to every creature," Mark 16:15; also Romans 10:9-10).

I CAN BE HIRED—NOT BOUGHT

My feelings on what I say in a speech are quite clear. When anyone buys my services as a speaker, they buy me at my very best for that occasion. My best effort comes when I turn the talk over to the Lord. It would be unthinkable for me not to make reference in some way to Jesus Christ because I would not be at my best. In addition, my Christian brothers are encouraged and there is always the chance that my witness will be used by God to bring one or more people into a personal relationship with Jesus Christ. The total time I spend witnessing seldom exceeds one or two minutes, but since I speak at about 280 words per minute—with gusts up to about 550—I can cover a lot of territory in a matter of seconds. I feel quite strongly that God is encouraging me to continue witnessing in my talks because He is blessing the witnessing in many ways. Since program chairmen generally book me only after they have personally heard me or one of my recordings and since my publicity material identifies me as a Christian, I feel they know what my talk will include. I'm confident that my refusal to be a puppet on a string has cost me some engagements. I'm even more confident that for every engagement I lose by witnessing the Lord gives me two to take its place. I'd be less than honest if I didn't admit I like the Lord's arithmetic.

Christ very clearly said that if we do not acknowledge Him here, He will not acknowledge us there (Matthew 10:32, 33). So the message is very, very clear and as I see it, I've got a great deal at stake. As I witness I inject humor into the message because I believe people respond positively to a "happy" Christian. Another reason I witness in some way in my public and private walk with the Lord is because Dr. Gene Allen, a dedicated Christian dentist in Dallas, showed me a card which asked a provocative question: If it were against the law to be a Christian, would there be enough evidence to convict you? Since that day I have daily sought to build the evidence against me so if I am ever brought to trial for being a Christian (if you think that possibility is far-fetched, you'd better get your Bible and do some *more* studying), it would be impossible to select the necessary twelve men or women for the jury who were not already completely convinced I was "guilty as charged."

I'll never forget, after one seminar, when one man came to me and said he had gotten the "feeling" I was a Christian. My

142 CONFESSIONS OF A HAPPY CHRISTIAN

response to him was that if all he got was a feeling, then I definitely had to "clean up my act," because I never wanted to leave anybody in doubt as to where I stand on the matter.

BILLY GOAT CHRISTIANS

Many times I have program chairmen ask me if I get nervous or uptight before I speak. For a time I felt that it sounded a little vain to say it didn't bother me or make me nervous to stand in front of large audiences and speak for an hour or more. However, since I don't get fearful or nervous—and since I know *why* I don't get nervous—I quietly say to the chairmen, "No, I don't get nervous because I have been preparing for today all of my life. More importantly, I have turned this talk over to the Lord. I asked Him to give me a message, and I will simply deliver it. I'm confident that He will give me the message."

I believe every Christian can figure out a way to regularly get in a commercial for the Lord in the regular routine of his work or business. The basic problem is that we have too many "Billy Goat" Christians who are always "butting" things by saying, "I would witness, but . . ." Or, "I would tithe, but . . ." Or, "I would teach a Sunday school class, but . . ." Or, "I would conduct a Bible study in my home, but . . ."

HOW DO YOU TELL 'EM?

For many years I have been a professional salesman, sales trainer, and motivational speaker. One of my areas of specialization has been the creation of customized material for a number of different companies. Upon my acceptance of the Lord, it was laid on my heart that although Christians have the greatest product in the world to sell, we have done an absolutely miserable job of selling it. When I became "sold" on salvation through Jesus Christ I wanted everyone else to share the good news of eternity. Since the Lord in the Great Commission clearly tells us to "Go ye therefore into all the world, teaching and preaching," I felt that not only was I instructed to do so but I wanted to do so. As a believer I felt I needed through my own life to be an example of my belief.

One of the first things I teach salespeople is that selling is a "transferrence of feeling." If the salesperson can make the prospect feel about the product like he, the salesperson, feels about the product, then the prospect will be far more likely to buy that product. Rather obviously, the salesman must have that feeling before he can transfer it. As Willa Dorsey, the Negro spiritual singer, so beautifully says, "Brother, if you're gonna be convincing, you gotta be convinced!" (Incidentally, until you've seen and heard her sing "Peace in My Soul," you have missed one of the real spiritual highs of life.)

I was convinced about the merits of Jesus Christ, but to be honest, I had seen some Christians who, through ineptness, ignorance and misguided efforts, had done an ineffective job of witnessing for the Lord. Don't misunderstand. I know that God's Word does not return void. But there's a difference between being almost empty (void) versus being overflowing, and it has been my prayer that my words would be overflowing so that others could share the benefits I was receiving. So I prayed for guidance in witnessing.

In retrospect, I'm convinced that God has been preparing me all of my life for what I'm now doing. As a speaker, I am in front of over a half million people each year. I talk to a lot of people individually, but most of my work is in front of groups that generally exceed one thousand in number and go as high as seventeen thousand. I feel my greatest witnessing opportunity is in group situations, but I know it's an area that needs to be handled with prayer and sensitivity. The witnessing needs to be in good taste because it is difficult to influence and offend at the same time; therefore, I prayed fervently for the words to witness effectively. I also promised the Lord that I would not speak to any group, anywhere, at any time about any subject that I did not get in a commercial for Him.

LORD, WHAT ARE WE GOING TO DO?

Almost immediately I was presented with a real challenge. I was on a program with a particularly gifted speaker who had a great deal to say and who said it extremely well. The audience was "with him all the way." About two-thirds of the way into his talk he skillfully led the audience into sharing his views on transcendental meditation (TM); then he asked the audience if anybody was familiar with it. A number of hands went up. He then asked, "What do you think about it?" One lady shouted from the audience that it had changed her life and received a round of applause for the statement. I sat there in shock and disbelief and wondered what to do to combat this effective presentation of a Far Eastern religion. (In the "old" days, I had a trite saying: "When in doubt—don't." In other words, do nothing. The "new" me says, "When in doubt—or when not in doubt—ask the Lord.")

So, I started talking to the Lord. "Lord, what are we going to do? I cannot let this go unanswered when I speak. And yet if I'm not careful, I will offend some people. This man is a charmer and the crowd is with him." The speaker was making some unusual promises of better health, longer life, and relieving tension, with peace of mind as the prime objective. So I prayed for words to use. Almost immediately—as a matter of fact, before the speaker finished—the Lord had instructed me what to say.

My talk that day was on sales training. One segment of the talk dealt with teaching sales people how to ask questions. We know if a salesman asks questions, he uncovers needs and many times is able to lead the prospect to a decision. When the prospect answers the questions the natural result is an uncovering of his need for the goods or services being offered. I gave several examples of how to ask questions. Then I said to the audience, "Many of you undoubtedly wonder where you can get further instructions on how to ask questions, and I'm delighted to tell you there is now a manual available which gives you a very solid foundation for learning how to ask questions. It is called the Holy Bible. I would like to stress this has nothing to do with your religious beliefs, whether you have them or do not have them. The best "manual" on how to ask questions ever written is the Bible. Any fair-minded individual will agree that its author Jesus Christ was the greatest salesman who ever lived. He was also the greatest sales trainer who ever lived. He took twelve men—and one of them was a loser—and spread the Gospel in short order throughout the civilized world. If you will secure a red-letter edition of the Bible, meaning the words of Christ are in red, you will discover whenever Christ was asked a question he always answered it with a question or a parable. So, if you want to know how to ask questions, read your Bible."

Then I paused and smiled at the audience as I said, "And as long as you're reading the question, you might as well go ahead and read the answer because one of these days He is going to ask *you* a question. And if you get it right, you get to stay!" At that point the audience laughed. Then I looked straight at the other speaker and said, "Not only will it give you peace of mind now, but to tell you the truth, it will keep the heat off you later!" The audience roared, and I said, "Thank you, Lord."

IS THE HYPOCRITE CLOSER TO GOD THAN YOU ARE?

The experience was so exciting and rewarding I simply said, "Lord, what we need to do is work out a 'spiritual sales presentation' that would fit all the talks I make." As far as I was concerned that particular example fit the sales training situations, so my next project was a witness to cover the motivational situations. The Lord gave me another example. When I was writing my book *See You at the Top*, I was in the process of losing thirty-seven pounds. In the book, I describe in considerable detail how this took place. Then, as I was making talks around the country, I told the story and used this little analogy.

I stated in *See You at the Top* that you can go where you want to go, do what you want to do, and be like you want to be, but as I looked down and saw the forty-one-inch waistline and 202 pounds of Ziglar, I recognized that it would be hypocritical for me to do all that positive talking and writing about being like you want to be and then come waddling out on the stage at 202. So, I injected in a talking-to-myself routine the question, "Suppose somebody asked me if I believed what I had written?" Rather obviously, I would say, "Yes, I do." Then I could imagine them poking me in that forty-one inch waistline and asking me if I believed *all* of what I had written. Since at that point it would be rather obvious that I had not believed to the degree that I'd done anything about it, I raised the question: Was I a hypocrite? Then I would answer the question by saying, "Don't accuse me of being a hypocrite because nobody likes hypocrites!" As a matter of fact, I would say, "There are a lot of people who say they don't go to church because there's a bunch of hypocrites there. Of course," I would continue, "when someone makes a comment like that, I always smile and explain if a hypocrite is standing between you and God, it just means the hypocrite is closer to God than you are." So you are choosing between spending some time *here* with a few hypocrites or *all* your time hereafter with lots of hypocrites. (I know I won't do it, but I'm tempted to tell them to come to church anyhow because having one more there won't make that much difference.)

Without exception, the audience will at least chuckle pleasantly, and in most cases they will laugh out loud. Then I'll smile again and say, "As a matter of fact, in order to hide behind something, you've got to be smaller than what you're hiding behind." Generally speaking, there's more laughter. Then I say, "I also get amused at people who say they would read the Bible but they don't understand it. Of course, I've always felt that it's not the part of the Bible they *don't* understand that bothers them." (Pause, generally punctuated with laughter.) "Actually, God speaks very clearly. For example, I'll bet all of you have noticed that He did not call them 'The Ten Suggestions'. (More laughter.) Then I smile again and say, "Read your Bible. It's easy to understand if you'll ask the Author to guide you in it. And He is always available."

NO EDUCATION IS NO EXCUSE

My older brother, who finished the seventh grade, preached God's Word for thirty-three years and was used by God to lead hundreds into the Kingdom. He learned the Bible by the light of a kerosene lamp, sitting by the fireplace until long past midnight, night after night, year after year. His knowledge and understanding of the Bible could have come only through his diligent efforts and God's revelation. He has the knowledge in his head and the feeling in his heart. I'm convinced that in a debate with professional Bible students who believe that part of the Bible is inspired by God and part is not and that they have been inspired to pick out the uninspired, he would more than hold his own. Many times I have people come forth and say I have missed my calling, that I should have been a preacher. I find this both flattering and very humorous because, even though I'm not preaching, I am spreading the Word. As I understand it, that's what preachers are also supposed to do. In my particular case, I have opportunities to witness to thousands of people who never get inside a church. The same, dear reader, is true of you. While you might not have an audience of thousands, you regularly have an audience of one or more. Don't misunderstand. I don't believe you're supposed to witness to everybody all the time. But I do believe there are occasions, virtually every day of our lives, when each of us has an opportunity to let people know our faith is in the Lord.

Sometimes I'm amused, and sometimes a little provoked, at the Christians who think that all they've got to do is set a good example, live a good life, and never publicly confess the Lord. A simple reading of Romans 10:9 will clearly establish that God expects us to *tell* people about Him. I believe the following example of what an impact one person can have clearly spells out our responsibility to spread the Word to one—or many. I heard this example from Dr. Adrian Rogers, pastor of the Bellevue Baptist Church in Memphis, Tennessee. I shall never forget the first time I heard this man of God speak. He was tall, handsome, articulate, and athletic-looking, with a voice that demanded attention because you knew he was God's messenger with God's Word.

YOU ARE TOO IGNORANT

In 1855 a Sunday school teacher named Kimbell laid a trembling hand on a nineteen-year-old shoe clerk and told him about salvation and Jesus Christ. The shoe clerk bowed his head and asked Christ to come into his life. He attempted to join the church, but they turned him down because he was too ignorant. A year later they finally admitted him and he became a Sunday school teacher. God used him so effectively that he was invited to go to England to preach. His name was Dwight L. Moody and he preached in the church of an imposing, well-educated, and cultured theologian named Frederick B. Meyer. Moody murdered the King's English and told deathbed stories. He told one real tear-jerker about how a Sunday school teacher discovered he was dying of cancer and led every member of his class to the Lord. As Moody preached, Meyer squirmed. He was upset that Moody would preach such a sermon. Later, Mr. Meyer asked one of the ladies from the choir how things were going. With a tremendous burst of enthusiasm she said, "Tremendous since Mr. Moody was here. I have led every member of my Sunday school class to the Lord."

THE LANGUAGE OF THE SOUL

Meyer said on that day, for the first time, he learned the language of the soul. Later, F. B. Meyer came to the United States for an evangelistic tour. On one occasion when he was preaching, Wilbur Chapman, a discouraged young minister, was in the audience. The Spirit of God moved through F. B. Meyer to Wilbur Chapman, and he became one of the outstanding evangelists in our country. As Chapman's ministry grew, he needed an assistant to handle details and do much of the work. The young man he selected was a former baseball player who was working at the YMCA. His name was Billy Sunday, and he had only a high school education. However, it was said that Billy

Sunday, following in Wilbur Chapman's footsteps, led over one million people to Jesus Christ.

In Charlotte, North Carolina, in 1924, Billy Sunday preached a revival with such power and impact that a prayer group was formed. This prayer group regularly assembled for prayer. When the depression started, they were convinced it was part of God's judgment for the sinful ways of the nation. They specifically prayed that another revival be sent to Charlotte, North Carolina. In answer to this prayer, Mordecai Ham was sent. He was a fire-and-brimstone preacher who preached hell hot and heaven sweet. As he preached, a sixteen-year-old farm lad sat there and started to squirm. He even joined the choir so he could get behind Mr. Ham. However, God's Spirit moved and Billy Graham finally responded. He has preached to kings, presidents, and prime ministers throughout the world. God alone knows how many people he has led to salvation.

Yes, we never know what is going to happen, but we know we "pass it on." The intriguing thing is that it all started with a Sunday school teacher named Kimbell, moved to an almost illiterate shoe clerk, before a "talented, educated" person entered the picture. The story emphasized the point. Do the best you can with what you have and God will take what you've done and "pass it on." The interesting thing about the story is that the church members took over a year to agree that Dwight L. Moody could become a member. They simply felt that he was not qualified to accept Jesus Christ and be a member of that church. It then took him a longer period of time to get to be a Sunday school teacher. The rest, of course, is history.

My challenge to you is a simple one. Suppose there was a Dwight L. Moody next to you in the store, office, factory, or assembly line where you are working. If you knew he was another Dwight L. Moody, would you tell him about what it means to know Jesus (assuming you know the Lord)? The answer is obvious, there'd be no hesitation on your part. So my next question is also obvious: how do you know the person you commute with or live next door to or have lunch with or work next to is *not* another Dwight L. Moody or Billy Graham? God promises that His Word shall not return void. If knowing Jesus means a lot to you—and if you know Him it does—then let me urge you to pray for God's guidance so that you might witness effectively, and for God's courage so that you will witness often.

ANOTHER EXCITING ENTREE FROM GOD'S HEAVENLY SMORGASBORD

One tremendous area of misunderstanding as it relates to Christians has to do with fear. Many times Christians talk about fear, but not once, in any place, does the Bible tell us that we are to fear. As a matter of fact, it repeatedly tells us to "fear not." It also says, "Resist the devil, and he will flee from *you*." We fear not because, when you put on the whole armor of truth and hide behind Jesus Christ, we know in whom we've believed and are secure in that belief. With fear removed (I'm talking about unreasonable fear), our effectiveness and productivity increase greatly. This brings us lots of *now* benefits.

REMEMBER: The more you thank God for what you have, the more you will have to thank God for.

First "Thank You" Date _____

Second "Thank You" Date _____

THANK YOU, LORD

FOR:

1. _____
2. _____
3. _____
4. _____
5. _____
6. _____
7. _____
8. _____
9. _____
10. _____
11. _____
12. _____

The phrase "God said it, I believe it, and that settles it" is partially true. My friend, if God said it, that settles it, whether you believe it or not.

Confess faults one to another; confess sin only to God.

Walk with meekness — not weakness.

The meek shall inherit the earth; but in the original Greek, meek meant power — with restraint.

Realistically we can be happier and more enthusiastic about everything we do, provided we are doing it for Jesus.

When an immigrant comes to America, before he can become a citizen he must renounce all his commitments and allegience to his former homeland and pledge 100 percent allegience to America. Then and only then will the U.S. Government grant him citizenship. That's the way it is with Jesus. When you accept Christ as Lord and Savior, you renounce Satan completely. You can't "split time" by serving Satan part-time and Christ part-time.

If you haven't met Satan face to face, it's because you are running in the same direction.
Man may go to Heaven without Health
                    without Wealth
                    without Fame
                    without a Great Name
                    without Learning
                    without Big Earnings
                    without Culture
                    without Beauty
                    without Friends
                    without 10,000 other things;
But he can never go to Heaven without Christ!

CHAPTER TEN

An Open Mind and an Open Bible Will Make *You* a Christian

I'm always puzzled by the people who claim to be so logical and analytical in their approach to life. They explain they believe in evolution because it is logical, while the story of creation isn't. Interestingly enough, when I ask the same people what they think when they watch television and see a frog changed into a handsome prince, they always reply that it is obviously a fairy tale. And they *know* it is exactly that, a fairy tale, unless they give it a little more time. Then they call it evolution. The theory of evolution is refuted by nature itself. You can take a hundred thoroughbred horses, a herd of fine cattle, or a pack of pure bred dogs and turn them loose in an isolated area. Each species will *devolve* and in just a few generations become scrubs.

I am told on good authority that in the Louvre in Paris, you will find three and one-half *miles* of science books which are no longer used because they are no longer valid. Thousands upon thousands of scientific "facts," carefully thought through and *scientifically* proven are out of date a few years later when new scientific evidence "proves" the original facts weren't facts at all. Contrast that with God's perfect Word in which *no* scientist anywhere has ever found even one scientific error. Yet, there are those who claim to be "logical," who believe "science" but question God.

A WRISTWATCH ON THE MOON?

I love what Bill Glass, the former all-pro end for the Cleveland Browns and now an outstanding evangelist, has to say on the subject. Bill depicts the first two astronauts walking on the moon and stumbling over a wristwatch accurately and busily ticking away the correct time. The first one asked, "What's that?" The second one replied that it was a wristwatch. The first one countered, "But I thought we were the first men to walk on the moon." The second one assured him that, indeed, they were the first. Somewhat puzzled, the first astronaut said, "Well, if we're the first ones here, where did the watch come from?" A little out of patience, the second astronaut said, "It didn't start out as a watch," and went on to explain that he had a completely "logical" explanation for the existence of the watch. "Billions of years ago," he said, "there appeared a single molecule of iron which evolved, grew, changed, and refined itself into fine steel. Over the years it added springs, weights, jewels, balances, and a crystal. Originally it 'grew' a chain because it was a pocket watch, but man's needs changed, the chain receded, and a wrist band 'grew' in its place. So you see, my little astronaut buddy, that's the way this wristwatch got on the moon." Of course, that's not the way wristwatches "happen" any more than man "happened" to come from monkeys, despite the fact that some people think and act as if they did.

The real tragedy of teaching evolution as a theory—much less as a science—is the destructive impact it has on the self-image of people of all ages. Think about it. If *anyone* really believed he came from a monkey instead of being created in the image of God, doesn't it stand to reason he would think less of himself? Take two three-year-olds with essentially the same characteristics. Constantly tell one he came from a monkey. Tell the other one he was created in God's own image. Now, doesn't it make sense that the child who knows he was created in God's own image will have a better opinion of himself?

DID DARWIN DOUBT?

When Charles Darwin, the concocter of the theory of evolution, made his trip around the world on the ship, *Beagle,* he visited the southern tip of South America and the region of Tierra del Fuego. The people in that poverty-stricken land were so degraded morally, spiritually, intellectually, socially, and physically that Darwin thought he had discovered the missing link between the ape and Homo sapiens. He proclaimed to the world that these people were so debauched, degraded, and depraved that they had no moral sensitivity. They were like animals and were surely the missing link. The Christian people of England heard about the tragic condition of this tribe. The Church Missionary Society of London thereupon sent men of God to preach the Gospel to these natives. They turned to the Lord in repentance and in faith, and many of them became model Christians. Darwin was so astonished at the miracle of Christ which had been wrought in the hearts of those poor people that he became a regular subscriber to the Church Missionary Society. On his deathbed, Darwin acknowledged the existence of Almighty God. Surely the results these dedicated English Christians obtained when they preached Jesus to the missing link natives of Tierra del Fuego had an impact on him. *Question:* If Jesus can open the hearts and change the lives of these missing link natives, doesn't it make sense that He can do the same for you?

ENJOYMENT WITHOUT UNDERSTANDING

Once, while rushing to catch a plane in Oklahoma City, I made a wrong turn which delayed me enough to miss the plane. When this happened (it was in mid-1973), I had been serving the Lord long enough to know there was a reason for my taking the wrong turn which caused me to miss the plane, so I asked Him to reveal it to me. He directed me to the radio. A layman (I believe he was a sergeant in the U.S. Army) was talking about his faith and why it wasn't necessary to understand everything in order to enjoy and benefit from it. "For example," he said, "I've seen a cow, a chicken, and a sheep all eating green grass from the same pasture. The chicken takes that grass into her system and lays an egg. The cow eats the grass and gives milk. The sheep eats the grass and produces wool. Now, I don't have any idea how the cow, the sheep, and the chicken can take the same grass and produce entirely different products, but the most brilliant scientists don't really know, either. However, I can't recall anyone ever telling me he wasn't going to eat eggs, drink milk, or wear wool clothing because he doesn't understand how chickens convert grass to eggs, how cows convert grass to milk, or how sheep manufacture wool from grass."

Eggs, milk and wool are important, but they only satisfy our wants and needs temporarily. Jesus Christ, the Lamb of God, is the Bread of Life and provides the Living Water which quenches our thirst forever (John 6:35, 48; John 4:10, 11). Realistically, it doesn't make much sense to turn down a glass of milk because you don't understand how the cow produces it. Doesn't it make even less sense to turn down eternal life because you don't understand everything? Personally, I can't understand how God could love us so much that two thousand years before we were born He sent His Son into the world to die on the cross for the sins we were going to commit. But just because I don't understand that love doesn't mean I can't accept it.

NO SCIENTIFIC DISAGREEMENT

Don't misunderstand. There is overwhelming *scientific* evidence that the Bible is the Word of God, and there has *never been* a single disagreement or contradiction between science and the Bible. Science has been a little slow on many things, but eventually it will catch up.

FOR THE SCIENTIST, HERE IT IS, IN YOUR OWN LANGUAGE

As I was putting the finishing touches on this book, I was speaking in Atlanta. I made reference to the theory of evolution and its destructive impact on the self-image of our youth. Seated in the audience was Clinton J. Washam, Ph.D., an internationally recognized researcher from the University of Georgia with over fifty research papers among his long list of credentials. Dr. Washam visited with me after the session and I learned he was quite a man. He holds the black belt in Tackwondo and believes in creation as a scientist and as a Christian. As he expresses it, he came to this conclusion not to please man, mom, or minister, but through the processes God endowed him with. I was so intrigued with what Dr. Washam had to say that I asked him to put it in writing for me. He graciously agreed, and the next four paragraphs are his.

BE LEERY OF THE THEORY

Calculation of the volume of our planet earth yields a figure of approximately 4×10^{27} cubic centimeters. Calculation of the volume of an intestinal bacterial cell gives a figure of approximately one cubic micron. Therefore, the number of bacteria equivalent to the volume of the earth is 4×10^{39} cells. Please retain this concept as we continue to develop our thoughts. Now bacteria, being one-celled creatures, may have a generation time of 20 minutes. This means one cell may divide into two in 20 minutes, and two into four in an additional twenty minutes. The equivalent generation time for man is, perhaps, 20 years. If left to grow unchecked for 24 hours, the bacteria would undergo 72 generations, which is equivalent to 1,440 human years. At the end of this time the bacteria would still be recognizable and identifiable as duplications of the original single cell. This occurs in spite of the fact that the cell's DNA may contain at least 20 billion possible base sites for mutation. Developing this further, at the end of 48 hours there would be approximately 4×10^{42} bacterial cells as offspring resulting from one original cell. That mass of cells would equal 4,000 times the volume of the earth, but all of them would be bacteria. Not all would be alike, to be sure, but they would have reproduced "after their kind." Considering that less than 1×10^{10} humans have graced the surface of our planet in its entire history and that one year in a bacterial culture may be equivalent to 500,000 years of human life, how can I, as a logical scientist, swallow the camel of evolution and strain at the gnat of creation?

I had enough geology in my undergraduate training to know that the deeper a river, the harder it is to change its course. The river of evolution is fifty miles wide and one inch deep. In fact, it is more of a mucky swamp than a river. It must flow like a stream of sillyputty to conform to the ever changing multitude of theories and ideas. In contrast, the river of creation is immeasurably deep and straight. Its very depth causes some vision problems as one studies the mysterious abyss where the light of the Scripture was never intended to penetrate. However, the upper limits are profoundly clear, and it is these limits that touch our lives. How deep the river appears to you and me is, in part, determined by our parents and teachers (including television) when we are young. Each either clears the water to a greater depth or fills it with the rocks and dirt of evolution until it becomes a shallow, aimless thing.

Evolution is not only bad for the self-image, but is incorrectly presented as a scientific principle. It is not science, although scientists were the original architects and the first to embrace the theory. Evolution is not a system that is based on scientific principles. It is, in fact, history and, at that, history based on rather flimsy and scant, yet carefully selected, data. An evolutionary historian sifts through the mountain of nature's records and plucks out the pieces he wants, puts them in a small basket, and then arranges them into an ill-fitting picture. The picture poses few flaws to those with poor eyesight—the same poor eyesight that fails to see the remaining mountain of pieces and consider their place in the over-all picture. It is truly a modern reenactment of the blind men describing an elephant from the parts that each can feel.

It cannot be denied that microevolution does occur. Red cats do not always beget red kittens, but they do always beget kittens, not dogs. The poodle didn't exist a hundred years ago, and neither did Santa Gertrudis cattle, but their ancestors were truly "after their own kind." God did not create every creature just as you now find it. He did create the original kinds with their potential to adapt and adjust with time. However, just because my knit shirt has inbuilt flexibility and adaptation to limited stress, it does not suggest that the shirt would adapt to the physical form of a cow or a goat. At that point there would be an unattainable switch from microevolution to macroevolution. Evolutionists try to make the same switch.

THERE'S MORE, LOTS MORE

God told us in the Book of Isaiah that the world was a circle (Isaiah 40:22); two thousand years later man said, "Hey, this thing is round!" When God dictated the Book of Genesis to Moses, He moved Moses to write that He had created man from the dust (Genesis 2:7); thousands of years later the scientists discovered that the sixteen chemical elements that make up the human body also make up the dust of the earth, thus establishing the scientific feasibility of man coming from the dust.

God told us three thousand years ago that the life is the blood (Leviticus 17:11). Recently man confirmed this fact scientifically. Since the blood of man is different from the blood of animals, that fact alone disproves the theory of evolution. (If the blood weren't different, blood plasma in unlimited amounts could be acquired by regular visits to the slaughter house.)

Here's one that really blew my mind. Fifty men of God from three different continents wrote the sixty-six books of the Bible in three different languages covering a period of some fifteen centuries. Each book "fits" with the others like a hand fits in a glove, and there is not one single contradiction. If you don't think God had His hand in that miracle, then, my friend, you've never heard two people report the same traffic accident they had simultaneously observed from the same vantage point just five minutes earlier. The prophet Isaiah prophesied over seven hundred fifty years in advance that Christ would be crucified on a tree. At that time, Israel was not under subjection to Rome, and the *only* method of execution used in Israel was death by stoning.

DID GOD REALLY WRITE THE BIBLE?

Many times the skeptic or nonbeliever will approach me with a "you-can't-be-serious" expression when I state that I believe the Bible is literally true. My answer is a simple, "Yes, I do." Sometimes they will just give me a "poor fellow" shake of the head and go on their way. More often, they attempt to enlighten me by pointing out that the Bible is full of contradictions. When this happens, I always—as gently and courteously as possible— say to them, "I hope you won't think me rude or presumptuous, but with your permission I would like to finish the conversation by handling both sides of the discussion. If I misquote you I will apologize and ask your forgiveness. Is that fair enough?" (They generally are surprised but agreeable.) "You say the Bible is full of contradictions and I'm going to say, 'Show me one.' You're going to say, 'Well, I don't know where they are but it's full of them.' And I'm going to say, 'Show me one.'" This could go on forever, but I have never yet had anyone show me a single contradiction. The reason is simple and obvious. No contradictions exist in the Bible. The God who cannot lie cannot possibly contradict Himself.

CHRISTIANS HAVE POWER—AND AUTHORITY

Recently, while my redhead and I were in San Antonio celebrating our thirty-first wedding anniversary, we heard Dr. Sam Cannata, a medical missionary to Ethiopia. Dr. Cannata had been imprisoned for a short period of time during the turbulent change of administrations in Ethiopia. He is a dedicated man who makes a lot of sense. It's always encouraging to hear dedicated Christians from all walks of life share their experiences because they can draw analogies that are meaningful and often very different. Dr. Cannata pointed out that medicine and man always—ultimately—lose the battle against death, but knowing Jesus Christ enables us to live forever—in paradise.

Dr. Cannata also pointed out that God has given us the power of attorney through Jesus Christ. It's wonderful to know that we represent Him and that He has given us power to act in His name and with His authority. He also stressed that Satan has power, but no authority, and pointed out that a policeman can hold up his hand and stop a big truck weighing many tons because the policeman has authority over the driver. The driver has the *power* of hundreds of horses at his disposal in that powerful engine, but the power of the engine comes under the authority of the policeman. It's exciting to know that although Satan has power, he has no authority. Christ has given authority to all who believe and call on His Holy name.

DON'T CUT YOURSELF OFF FROM THE HEAD

Perhaps the clearest and most meaningful example Dr. Cannata used was that of people who have paralyzed legs. In most cases, there's nothing wrong with the legs, but the nerves have been cut off from the head. The nerves leading from the head are no longer connected to the legs. The same thing often happens to Christians. They are spiritually cut off from the head, Jesus Christ, and their conduct and performance is paralyzed. Generally speaking, most people who have paralyzed legs would do virtually anything to be able to walk again. Many times they could walk if they could make connection through the nerves to the head. They would love to make that connection, and yet, that connection from head to legs would only give them power over their legs. Millions of Christians, on the other hand, have disconnected themselves from the body of Christ by choice, indifference, or carelessness. Yet that connection to Christ would give them infinitely more power and benefits than the person with paralyzed legs could receive by connecting the nerves to the head. It's gloriously exciting to know that we can stay connected to the source of all power and authority just by opening our hearts and our minds to Him.

WHERE DO CHRISTIANS COME FROM?

A little boy watched a sculptor working diligently on a piece of marble and was amazed as a man emerged from the marble. When the work was completed, the little boy asked the sculptor, "How did you know a man was in that block of marble?" The sculptor replied that all he had done was knock away the part of the marble which did not look like a man. In the truest sense of the word, we could also say that inside every human being on the face of this earth there is a Christian waiting for someone to come along and chisel away until his mind and heart open and allow Jesus to come in. Many times people complain that God is not using them. God cannot do much through us until He gets *in* us. The moment Christ comes in, He then proceeds to chip away the parts which do not look like a Christian. Finally, the day comes when we see the born-again Christian, the person who will stand without blemish in front of the judgment seat of Christ.

A CHILD IS LOST

My friend A. C. Carlson, from Minneapolis, sends this thought: When we hear the words "a child is lost," a chill falls over many loving, caring people. Hundreds of people who do not know the child will throw themselves into the search for that lost one. Many of them forget all other responsibilities and search for hours, sometimes throughout the night. They look in the wilderness, on mountaintops, in waterways, and any other place where they feel the child might be. Yes, the words "a child is lost" sends chills through many compassionate people. Yet, as A. C. points out, we're living in a world where there are millions of lost people, some of them next door. These lost people surely rate as much love and concern as the lost child. Yet, somehow, because the urgency is not there, we have a great tendency to ignore the lost, especially if they are "lost" next door.

"CUSS," SWEAR, DRINK, AND SMOKE

About three years ago, while flying from Indianapolis, Indiana, to Salem, Oregon, to fill a speaking engagement, I was assigned a seat on the plane out of Chicago next to a stewardess with a broken leg. When I sat down she was reading. Since I had a great deal of work to do, I was pleased that she, too, was busy. However, when lunch was served, it was natural that we exchange pleasantries, which we proceeded to do. After about five minutes of conversation, she started spouting the most obscene and filthy language I have ever heard. Since she was taking the name of our Lord in vain, I knew I could not let it go unchallenged. I waited for the appropriate moment and asked God to lead the conversation so I could be an effective witness to the girl.

The opportunity came within minutes and I seized it by telling her that I had read a most surprising article in one of the magazines. A firm in New York conducts seminars teaching women how to get ahead in business. They maintain that femininity and tears are no longer acceptable in a "man's" world. They contend if a woman is to get ahead, she must smoke, drink, cuss, and swear like a man. I explained to my seatmate this was especially shocking because every man I know is firmly of the opinion that a woman's most effective weapons or tools of persuasion are her charm and femininity, and that tears are an integral part of the female arsenal. I explained that, in my own particular case, my redhead already gets everything she wants. But turning on the tears is like shooting a bird on the ground. It is unfair and should be declared illegal, or at least immoral. The tears remove all doubts and barriers and greatly speed the acquisition process. I also mentioned that when a woman acts "like a man" (though how anybody could equate profanity, vulgarity, and boorishness with manhood is beyond my wildest imagination), I simply treat her as she is acting, which is "like a man". I also pointed out that most men can more effectively deal with other men than they can with a "defenseless" woman.

THEY'RE JUST WORDS

The stewardess was totally shocked and said she could not believe she was hearing what I was saying. Indignantly, she explained that they were just words. Then, using an old sales technique which I have found to be most effective, I repeated quietly and in questioning form, "Just words?" Whereupon the girl began to explain what she meant. After about three minutes she paused, looked at me, and said, "You know, what I'm saying doesn't make any sense, does it?" To which I grinned and replied, "No, it doesn't. But then I'm certain you talk that way in front of your parents and your little brother." She quickly protested, "Oh, no I don't." Then I smiled again and said, "Why not? They're just words!" At this we both laughed.

The conversation then turned to spiritual lines, and I asked her what would happen to her if our plane did not reach Salem, Oregon. She seemed puzzled by the question, so I asked if she knew where she would go when she died. She instantly and emphatically answered, "To Heaven." I asked her how she knew with such certainty she would go to Heaven. She explained that she was a "good person," had never done anything to harm anyone, and had tried to live by the Golden Rule. (Interestingly enough, this is pretty much a standard answer to the question about going to Heaven.) After a couple of moments of this, I looked at her and quietly said, "I'm convinced that my mother at this instant is comfortably seated in the presence of the Lord. However, I'm even more convinced that she is not there because of her goodness, though in my eyes she was truly a good and beautiful person." I explained that nobody, not even Billy Graham, the Pope, my mother, or Matthew, Mark, Luke, or John could get to Heaven because of their goodness. All have, according to Paul in Romans, "sinned and come short of the glory of God." There is none good, no, not one. Then she asked, "How do you get to Heaven?" I opened my Bible and turned to Ephesians and read from the second chapter, the eighth and ninth verses: "For by grace are ye saved through faith; and that not of yourselves: it is the gift of God; Not of works, lest any man should boast."

WHO DID WRITE THE BOOK?

Her retort was that the Bible was written by men, and that therefore it was not a reliable yardstick. I've established some of the reasons why I believe the Bible is true so I won't repeat them here, but I looked at the girl and asked her if she were a sports fan. She assured me she was. She specifically told me she was a Pittsburgh Steelers fan and especially a Terry Bradshaw fan. She also pointed out that she had just won a bet on them. With this bit of knowledge, I asked her a question: "Suppose Terry Bradshaw (quarterback for the Pittsburgh Steelers) were to announce in preseason that he was going to throw six thousand consecutive passes and complete them all, that none of them would be dropped, there would be no errors and not one of them would be intercepted." How would she bet on the six thousand completions?

She stated she'd bet everything she had that he could not do it. Then I asked, "Suppose he were to throw thirty-nine passes in the first preseason game and all of them were completed. What would you think?" She responded that she'd feel he had a hot hand for that game. Then I said, "Well, suppose at the end of the exhibition season he'd thrown seven hundred fifty completions without an interception, without a single one being dropped. Then what would you think?" She replied, "I would begin to get a little nervous about my bet." I pursued it by saying, "Suppose he threw three thousand, one hundred and nine consecutive completions. When he faded back for number three thousand, one hundred and ten, how would you bet on that toss of the ball?" She enthusiastically responded, "I would bet everything I had he would complete the next one!"

YOU'RE BETTING YOUR LIFE

Then, laying my hand on my Bible, I looked at her and said, "You're looking at a book of prophecy in which God prophesied over six thousand future events. Over three thousand of them have already taken place without error, complete in every detail. One of the things He has prophesied is that Jesus Christ will come again. My question to you is simply this: Are your ready to meet Jesus? Are you prepared to bet your eternal soul that after more than three thousand completions, the Lord is going to drop the ball?" He explains in His Book there is no way any of us can know when He is coming, but that we should be ready at anytime. The question I asked the young stewardess is the same I ask you as a reader: If the Lord were to come at this moment, do you know and *know* that you know that you would go home with Him? It's one thing to bet a few pennies or a few dollars on a football game, though I feel gambling is wrong, but it's an entirely different matter to bet your eternal soul the Lord is not coming again, or that He is going to delay the trip until *you* are ready for Him to come.

Much to my dismay, the girl did not make a decision for the Lord. To the best of my knowledge, she still has not. Though I have continued to send her materials, I have never gotten a response. She will receive this book, and if she reads these words maybe it will bring back memories to her. Since God promised so clearly in His Book that His words would not fall void or return empty, I'm convinced one reason He put me on that airplane was for the purpose of talking to that girl. I also believe He gave me this particular analogy for your benefit as well as hers. I say this for two reasons: first of all, after flying nearly two thousand miles at my own expense to make a speech (I had to pay my own expenses because the airport was fog bound and we couldn't land for me to make the speech); secondly, in my talks around the country I often use the football analogy, and many people have said it was an eye opener for them. It has also helped to clarify my own thinking.

I'M NOT TRYING TO "PROVE" GOD

Don't minunderstand—I'm not trying to "prove" God. I love what Billy Graham said in one of his columns: "Remember that only love can really "see" God—not the intellect. It's not that the eternal existence of God is contrary to reason. It is rather beyond reason." That's why Paul in Ephesians 1:18 talks about "the eyes of your heart." Incidentally, Jehovah God is the *only* God who wrote one— and only one— book of prophecy. He wrote it, and He published millions of copies in hundreds of languages. Despite every conceivable effort by Satan and his cohorts, it still lives and heads the best-seller list *every* year. Buddha, Mohammed, and other "prophets" and "gods" never wrote a book of prophecy because just *one* mistake would expose them for what they are— false gods or false prophets.

If there are other gods or prophets who *know* everything past, present, and future, why didn't they write a book and tell us what was going to happen in the next year, not to mention the next thousand or so years? A prime example of twentieth century prophets can be found in the daily horoscope and in people such as Jeanne Dixon, who claims to get her messages from God. Incredibly enough, millions of people read the horoscope religiously while laughingly maintaining that it "just gives them something to do," and "of course, they don't believe it!"

Three thoughts: one, we know Jeanne Dixon and the other astrologists do not get their information from God because God makes no mistakes, and Jeanne Dixon's predictions are wrong much of the time. The most notable example came when she confidently predicted that Jackie Kennedy wasn't about to marry anyone. The *next* day Jackie married Aristotle Onassis. Two, God tells us that the horoscope and its advocates are of Satan. When you read the daily horoscope, you are reading Satan's daily bulletin, published in hell (Isaiah 47:13 and the Book of Daniel). Three, if you claim any degree of practicality, think about this for a moment: the "science" of astrology is founded on the belief that the sun revolves around the earth. The evidence is overwhelming that astrology is satanic and, yet, there is no denying that many of the astrologists are amazingly accurate in their predictions. Jeanne Dixon for example seems to know things the average man or woman could not know, but she does make mistakes. *Question:* If she knows more than man knows but obviously less than God knows, where does the information come from? A moment's thought will give you the answer, won't it? But for the few of you who miss it, the answer is Satan. He is the second most knowledgeable being in existence. In the battle for your soul, second place or second choice is hell—literally.

WHEN WERE YOU BORN?

Many times, after a speaking engagement, someone will come to me and say, "When were you born?" I know what they're getting at, so I generally use one of two approaches. Sometimes I say, "Which time? The time which started my life or the time which changed my life?" The response varies, but generally they say, "No, when were you *actually* born?" Then I will say, "In 1926." By then some of them begin to get a little exasperated and say, "No, I mean what month?" Then I will say, "Oh, you want to know the *sign* under which I was born!" And they say,

"Yes." Then I say, "I was born under the sign of the Cross." They respond, "Naw, come on, tell me, what month and day?" Then I very seriously say to them, "That's information you don't need, and if I give it to you I will be feeding a tool of Satan." Unfortunately there are many Christians who deliberately, on a daily basis, walk into Satan's den to read his bulletins. Many times this is the first step into involvement with the ouija board, the occult, and Satan-worship itself. My advice concerning the horoscope can be summed up in one simple word— *"don't."*

I shall never forget a little lady who came to me and, with much enthusiasm, asked, "When were you born?" And I said, "July 4, 1972." She obviously did not hear the "1972," as she started rattling off, "I knew it, I knew it, you have every characteristic of a . . ." and then she named the satanic sign of those who are born on July 4. "You are . . .," and then she started rattling off a long list of qualities. I quietly kept my peace and let her rave on as I waited for her to finally stop. Eventually she did. Then I looked at her and said, "You did not hear the rest of my statement. That birthdate was July 4, 1972. At that time I was born *again.* Now, my mother got me here on November 6, 1926." Incredibly enough, the dear lady never batted an eyelash. She instantly started saying, "Well, that figures, because you have . . ." such and such, and such and such, and she proceeded to identify the characteristics of the people who are born on November 6. The dear lady never got the point that she was totally contradicting herself. Fortunately, those around her instantly recognized the fallacy of astrology and that it definitely is not a science.

I believe that if my date of birth had anything to do with the way I am, it would be unfair and completely un-Christlike, because there is nothing we can do about that *first* birthday. By the same token, I believe that my second birthday has *everything* to do with my conduct and nature. This is not a matter of opinion. My friends and relatives will tell you that the Zig Ziglar who was born on November 6, 1926, and the Zig Ziglar who was born again on July 4, 1972, are two entirely different people. Praise God!

GOD DID IT!

In 1977, as part of a baseball chapel program, I had the opportunity to speak to several of the major league teams, including the world champion New York Yankees. After the service, one of their pitchers who was a new Christian came to me for a brief conversation. He explained that he had expected to have a great year, but God had hurt his arm and the year had been frustrating and disappointing. He asked me if I thought God had hurt his arm as a way of telling him to get out of baseball. In one form or another this question is asked by Christians and non-Christians alike on an almost daily basis. Why did God make me sick? Why did God get me fired? Why did God tempt me? In simple terms, God *did not* hurt the young pitcher's arm, nor did He do any of the other things mentioned.

It's true that *everything* that happens has crossed God's desk *before* it happens, and He thus permits certain things to happen. But God does not do it. The guilty party is Satan and/or *you*. Example: a dedicated Christian has a stroke. A casual glance reveals that the victim was grossly overweight, which caused the high blood pressure which led to the stroke. You can't expect God to give you good health when you deliberately break His laws. God's laws work *all* of the time, not just some of the time, and they work whether you believe in them or not. This is definitely to our advantage, as my Christian brother and fellow speaker Skip Ross points out. Otherwise, we would wake up each morning wondering whether the law of gravity was in effect for the day or not. Can you imagine the frustration of not knowing whether your feet were going down or up when you stuck them over the side of the bed?

Yes, God's laws work—*For* you if you are with them and *Against* you if you violate them. You can't *waste* your money and expect God to reward you financially. You can't abuse your friends and family and expect admiration from strangers. You can't take advantage of others and not ultimately be taken advantage of. You can't burn the candle at both ends and not end up with difficulties directly related to that candle-burning. As you sow, so also shall you reap. The thing Christians have going for them is that "all things work together for good to them who love the Lord (when life hands you a lemon—make lemonade!). When misfortune strikes and you *know* there is a reason for it and you know you are in God's will, you react and deal with it in a different and far more effective way. Again I remind you that God did not promise us a trouble-free, griefless life. He did promise us that "all our sins and griefs He would bear," if we will take it to the Lord in prayer.

I JUST DON'T KNOW

The most difficult thing to explain—if in fact it can be explained—*and* the most difficult to understand—if it can be understood—is a tragedy involving an innocent, often helpless, individual: the rape and murder of a child, a plane crash involving many innocent people, a hit-and-run death, the mugging of an elderly cripple, a child taken by leukemia, a fatal traffic accident caused by a drunken driver. The list is endless, and in one way or another touches virtually every family in America. Rivers of tears have been shed, and the inevitable "Why? Why? Why?" goes unanswered. My own pastor recently celebrated his fiftieth anniversary as a minister. He truly loves the Lord and is a true student of the Bible, yet he shakes his head and says he doesn't really know why these things happen. It is, as he says, a mystery. One thing, however, stands out like a beacon. When good things happen—like development of a new wonder drug, an athlete breaking a record, or a person's business grows and prospers—mankind generally has an explanation for it. *I* studied hard and conducted hundreds of experiments, or *I* trained hard, or *I* worked hard. Mankind is all too often inclined to take credit for *his* accomplishments, but when things go wrong he blames God.

DEATH—WHERE IS THY STING?

Yet, even in tragedy, God through His Word offers hope for those who seek and believe. It starts with the promise of a better tomorrow, of life everlasting, of eternal peace. It's called faith,

and it offers hope where none existed. It certainly doesn't eliminate—and on occasion it might not even appear to reduce—the
grief, but from the depths of my being I can tell you that the
grief is totally different and far less devastating.

I would never use the word "relevant" when I speak of a
tragic death, but I use the word with conviction as it applies to
love and to grief. I've loved as a Christian and as a non-Christian
and observed love as it applies to both Christian and non-Christian. There is a difference. It's not that the non-Christian loves
less, but simply that the Christian, through Jesus Christ has a
capacity to love infinitely *more*. I've known grief through death
as a Christian and as a non-Christian. I have observed grief
through death among other Christians and non-Christians.
There is a difference. The non-Christian displays a grief of
despair, of hopelessness, and of helplessness—a grief that often
hints of bitterness, unfairness, and a "what am I going to do
now?" kind of frustration. It smacks of thwarted dreams and
gives the impression of "it's all over now" for those who are left
behind. The Christian's grief is actually deeper because the love
through Christ is deeper, but it's a different kind of grief. It's an
"I'll miss you deeply because I love you deeply" kind of grief.
It's different because the Christian knows that the separation
will be over in "the twinkling of an eye," as God measures time.
It's different because of trust that the Jesus who created the
universe is in control. We trust our living Savior with our lives
and the lives of our loved ones. It's different, though the tears
might be the same, because there is no despair, no helplessness,
no hopelessness. It's different because the Christian knows that
the departed brother or sister has gone to a better life, and we
know they are secure and happy. This is a tremendous comfort
and enables us to ultimately shed our grief and say, "Death,
where is thy sting?"

REMEMBER: The more you thank God for what you have, the more you will have to thank God for.

First "Thank You" Date _____

Second "Thank You" Date _____

THANK YOU, LORD

FOR:

1. _____

2. _____

3. _____

4. _____

5. _____

6. _____

7. _____

8. _____

9. _____

10. _____

11. _____

12. _____

If you are a Christian, even your dog should know it.
PROF. LUIS PANTOJA

CHAPTER ELEVEN

Just a Coincidence

A number of years ago two small boys from a remote rural area were placed on a passenger train to visit relatives in an adjoining state. Their parents gave each one of them a sack lunch and a dollar to spend on the trip. At the first stop about a hundred miles from home a vendor selling peanuts, candy, and popcorn came through the railroad car the boys were on. He was also selling bananas and since the boys had never tasted a banana, they decided to venture out and try something new. As luck would have it, the man across the aisle also bought one and started peeling it, so the older of the two boys did the same thing. When he had peeled it about halfway back, the little fellow took the obvious step, which was a big, big bite. At that precise moment the train pulled into a short but very dark tunnel. From bright daylight to total darkness took about a tenth of a second. As they pulled out of the tunnel the older boy saw his younger brother about to put his banana in his mouth. The older boy immediately grabbed his little brother's arm and shouted, "Don't eat that banana because it will strike you blind!"

Of course, that obviously *was* a coincidence, but since that July 4, 1972, the date when I turned my life over to the Lord, I have had a series of "coincidences" that were obviously not coincidences.

GOD KNOWS MY NEEDS

I had a need for a born-again Christian educator to work closely with me personally and to produce a teaching manual

173

and guide for a motivational self-help course for schools, churches, and businesses. This person had to be versatile and willing to do what needed to be done, whether the task was menial or prestigious. I planned to advertise in some Christian publications for this special person. The day before I intended to place the ad, my telephone rang. It was Carroll Phillips, who filled the spot quite well. The cynic would say, "So what?" But God said He knew my need *before* I voiced it. If I believe *in* God then I've got to believe God's Word.

FLIGHT CANCELLED

One Saturday I was scheduled to conclude a seminar in Minneapolis at noon and catch a 2:00 P.M. flight back to Dallas. On Friday the airline called and announced the cancellation of my return flight. No reason was given. They booked me and my associate, Carroll Phillips, whom by "coincidence" I had decided to take with me at the last minute, on a return flight at 3:20 P.M. I grumbled a bit since I am always anxious to get home, especially on Saturday, and the 3:20 flight made three stops, whereas the 2:00 P.M. flight was nonstop.

I spoke on Friday evening and as usual got in my commerical for the Lord, but in my mind there was nothing that set the occasion apart. Because the Saturday session started a little late and ran overtime, I felt a sense of relief at the departure delay. When I finished speaking I went to the booth to autograph books and help Carroll with the sale of our cassette recordings. At about 2:25 P.M. we were winding things up to head for the airport, which was twenty minutes away. One of the ladies who helped handle the seminar came to me and told me my message of the night before had "gotten to" a girl and her husband who were having marital and drinking problems. She asked if I would talk with them privately. A quick glance at my watch and a word from Carroll that he could handle the merchandise was all I needed to know. The lady, the young wife, and I headed upstairs to visit with the husband. By now it was 2:30 P.M. and we had to leave no later than 2:50 P.M. The husband, who did not know I was coming, was embarrassed when we entered the room, but he was very open and willing to accept any possible help from anyone.

INVITING JESUS IN

As I looked at the young man and his wife, it struck me they had their lives and the lives of their two young children in front of them. I prayed and prayed hard that God would send His Holy Spirit to direct my every thought, word, and action for the next few minutes. Much of what happened has been blotted from my memory. I remember telling them of God's great love for them, of His personal interest in their problems, and of His willingness to forgive and erase sins from the record book. I explained His deep interest in the preservation of the family and of the benefits of a sober mother and father raising the children together. I told them of the enormous difference it makes when you invite Jesus Christ into your heart. I shared with them the fact that all areas of my own family life were better and richer since my wife and I had invited Jesus into our lives and had given Him ownership and control. I confessed to them our own greatly increased love and happiness. At this point the wife, with tears streaming down her face, stated that she did not know how to invite Jesus into her heart. The Lord then led me to explain it would be like a close friend knocking on the door of your house. You would simply open the door and invite him to come in. Then I asked both husband and wife if they wanted to invite Jesus to come into their hearts and take over their lives. They both assured me that they did, and with bowed heads they opened the doors of their hearts and invited Jesus Christ to take over their lives.

It was quite a coincidence that the 2:00 P.M. flight was cancelled so that the Lord would have me at the right spot at the right time, but the coincidence doesn't end there. Two days later the young couple was scheduled to fly to the West Coast to find a house because they had just gotten an exciting new business opportunity. By coincidence, Dick and Bunny Marks, the couple in charge of the seminar and born-again Christians, knew *one* minister who really preaches God's Word. By "coincidence," this minister lives in the town the young couple were moving to. Amazing, isn't it (to the nonbeliever, that is), how God works things out so that the right people are at the right place at the right time to do the right thing for His people.

A CONFUSED TONGUE

One of the most exciting things that ever happened to me as a young Christian took place while I was making a speech. It was in Los Angeles, and the audience was large (about twenty-five hundred) and friendly. When I said hello and opened with a "one liner," the response was tremendous, and I instantly felt that I had them in the palm of my hand. After about three minutes I had a feeling of total control and said to myself, "Zig, you've really got them!" Then the Lord confused my tongue. I heard myself—much to my surprise and dismay—saying things in reverse. For example, instead of saying, "I was going to town," I said, "I to going town was." The first time I did it I could not believe what I heard. The second time it happened I got the message—loud and clear. Immediately I prayed, "Lord, I'm sure sorry for my ego trip and misplaced notion that *I* was making this talk. If you will forgive me and straighten me out, I'll be very careful to keep you on the throne of my life from this moment on." Immediately my speech cleared up and I was off to the races again. The whole incident probably took no more than ten seconds, and I seriously doubt that half a dozen people were aware that anything unusual had happened. It was tremendously significant to me, though, because it came through beautifully clear that the Lord was interested in every word I spoke. How exciting to know that the Creator of the universe is listening in and helping write your material!

I know there are those who would say it was just "one of those things," or that I was just imagining things, or that everybody fouls up from time to time, or that it was "quite a coincidence, wasn't it?" *They* can say or *think* what they will. I *know* God spoke to me, and I'm grateful that He was in my heart so I would listen. Today, when I'm speaking and get a good response from the audience, I just say, "Thank you, Lord," and go right on talking with the full assurance I am being monitored and directed. From time to time I hear actors and musicians express excitement because their director is so creative and/or talented. If they are excited about a mere mortal directing them, you've got to know I *really* get turned on knowing the Creator of the universe has taken a personal interest in directing my personal performances—on and off the stage.

ENGAGEMENT CANCELLED

On Saturday, September 17, 1977, Bob Hansrote, an old and close friend from Lincoln, Nebraska, died of cancer. I was speaking on the West Coast when the news came and had a longstanding engagement to be in Michigan by noon on Monday, the 19th. However, the engagement—by coincidence—was cancelled just a few days earlier, and I was able to go to Lincoln and spend a few hours with Bob's family at a critical time. God used the occasion and the circumstances to draw several members of the family closer to Him.

JUST A BOWL OF FRENCH ONION SOUP

A friend whose marriage was in trouble called me one morning and told me his wife of over twenty years was going to leave him and wanted a divorce. He was heartbroken. He said he loved her very much, didn't believe God wanted them to go their separate ways, and asked for advice and prayers. I gave him as much encouragement as I could and told him I would send them some information, including a recording which might be helpful. A few days later I got another wake-up call, but this time both husband and wife were on the line. They were just bubbling. The husband expressed appreciation for my prayers, suggestions, and the material I sent them. They were back together physically, emotionally, and spiritually.

Then the wife took over the conversation. She, too, expressed appreciation for the material and the suggestions, but then she really got to the heart of the matter as she said, "All of that stuff was good, Zig, but let me tell you why we listened in the first place. You were unaware we were watching, but about three months ago we were in the Fairmont Hotel in Dallas when you and your redhead came in for a bowl of their famous French Onion Soup. We watched the entire procedure from start to finish. The way you two "carried on" was something beautiful to see. You were so wrapped up in each other you were oblivious to the fact anyone else even existed. The love you have for each other and the enjoyment you have in each other made us know that when you speak and write about love and the family you truly are coming from the heart. In other words, Zig, you and Jean set an example which we plan to follow."

What a thrill to know God used that occasion to bring a husband and wife back together. I remember the occasion well. It was Sunday evening after church. On one of those spur-of-the-moment things we decided to stop by for that bowl of soup, which my redhead thinks is the greatest. Isn't it exciting to know God used that bowl of soup and the "coincidence" of that couple being in the restaurant at that precise time to put a family back together?

GET OUT OF THE WAY, ZIGLAR

Not too long after my commitment to serve the Lord, it dawned on me as I dug into the Scriptures there were two people I desperately needed to "get right with." They had been business associates and we had parted under rather bitter circumstances. I was guilty of washing some dirty linen in front of people who should never have been involved. It took a time to get my spiritual foundation solid enough and my confidence high enough to make the calls—in other words, to get me out of the way so Christ could work through me. Finally, on Christmas Day, 1972, I called both the parties in question, acknowledged my error, and asked them to forgive me for what I had done. They both appreciated the call, accepted my apology, and assured me it was all over. I learned an additional lesson from the calls because human nature being what it is, I felt that I, too, had been wronged. The interesting thing is neither of the parties I called asked me to forgive them for anything they might have done. Again, this is human nature. I'm confident both felt I was the "bad guy" and I was about 100 percent at fault. Be that as it may, the Bible clearly says that until I forgive those who have wronged me and ask forgiveness from those whom I have wronged, my slate with the Lord will not be clean. Since I certainly didn't want *anything* standing between me and the Savior, I made those two painful phone calls and had a pleasant visit with both of them.

Let me show you the practicality of following Jesus and taking Him at His Word. When I obeyed God's Word, a financial—not to mention spiritual—door was opened which has meant thousands of dollars to my company. One check for several thousand dollars, by coincidence, came at a time of substantial need under unusual circumstances. One of America's major corporations had booked me for a series of talks several months in advance. For several reasons they wanted to get the cost on the current budget, so they asked if it would be all right to pay me in advance. It was. In thirteen years of addressing major companies this had never happened before, nor has it happened since.

THE GALLBLADDER THAT WROTE A BOOK

As I was writing my first book in March of 1974, my gallbladder acted up, and it took four days before the surgeon identified the problem. I hurt more during those four days than I've hurt the rest of my life combined. When the attack came and the operation was scheduled, it caught me with an incredibly busy schedule. Prior to my commitment to the Lord, I'm confident that I would have been moaning and groaning that "it couldn't have come at a worse time." However, I can say with complete honesty that aside from the fact that I had to cancel numerous engagements and disappoint a number of people, I never moaned and groaned a minute. As a matter of fact, had the surgery *not* come (by coincidence) when it did, I don't know how I would have found time to finish my book.

To say that the gallbladder attack was a blessing in disguise is a gross understatement. Among other things, I was pushing too hard and had scheduled entirely too much work. Later, Dr. H. Leo Eddelman, one of God's most faithful servants, pointed out that the Twenty-third Psalm does say, "He *maketh* me to lie down. . . ." Sometimes we do not use the good judgment God gives us, so He acts in our best interests.

Concerning that operation, for some reason it never occurred to me that my problem was serious and that I was in any danger. Amazingly enough, I never even prayed for my own recovery. In a way, I guess my faith was such that I knew God knew my needs as well as my problem and that He would take care of me. Later the surgeon told me the gallbladder had ruptured about four days earlier, and that an abscess had formed under my liver. He had been unable to remove the gallbladder. He also said I was a very lucky man. I thanked God for sparing me.

Three things are worthy of mention. Nine months prior to the attack (by coincidence), I had started a dieting and physical conditioning program and had lost thirty-two pounds. I was actually in better physical condition at that moment than I had been in twenty-five years. You could never persuade me God hadn't prepared me well in advance for the ordeal He *knew* I faced. Secondly, just two years earlier my wife had also had a gallbladder operation, and Dr. Ernest Poulos had been her physician. We both liked and respected him, so we asked Dr. Holt, our family physician, to call him. Dr. Holt told us Dr. Poulos no longer performed abdominal surgery but nevertheless, he would ask. Happily, Dr. Poulos agreed to perform the operation. In my heart I know my wife's surgery two years earlier was also part of God's plan to involve Dr. Poulos, who is not only a superb surgeon but a man of God as well. Thirdly, my family, with my loving wife leading the way, was a constant source of support, and their prayers were many and fervent. My friends at the church—from the pastor to many of the members of the Sunday school class—were interceding in my behalf. So many of those dear people are prayer warriors of such total conviction that even as I write these words from high up in the air aboard an aircraft, my eyes are full and my heart is overflowing with the love of our Savior and the care and compassion of His servants.

SWEET HOUR OF PRAYER

After that first operation, I had a two-month wait before Dr. Poulos could operate again to remove the gallbladder. The second operation was relatively uneventful, but during the recuperation period I was able to put the finishing touches on my book and shortly thereafter get it to the printer.

During this period I had another beautiful and exhilarating experience with the Lord. Since I couldn't go to church, I was on the sofa watching Oral Roberts before our own televised services came on. In his simple and direct way, Oral was talking directly to my heart that Sunday morning. Again, the Lord knew my needs and filled them. That Sunday Oral's son, Richard, and his daughter-in-law, Patti, sang "Sweet Hour of Prayer," which was my mother's favorite song. I sat there drinking in the beauty of the words and, as my friend Jimmy Draper would say, "God broke a honey jug in my heart!" A moment later Jean walked in and embraced me on the sofa. Surely no man ever felt closer to his wife or loved her more than I loved my redhead—through Jesus Christ—at that instant. When you love God, I believe it is an impossibility *not* to love your family and your fellow man more. At that moment a thought that Dick Van Dyke had so beautifully expressed about marriage came to me. Dick observed that some people regard the rules of marriage as a prison to keep you from enjoying certain things. However, the happy ones feel that marriage provides a fence to protect the person and the things you hold most dear. I confess this is the way I feel about my marriage and my Lord. He is my shield and protector—my "fence" that stands between me and mine, and those forces which would do us harm.

I might add that this is not just the *Confessions of A Happy Christian*. The principle applies in all areas of life. Christ doesn't restrict our freedom. He extends it. A guardrail on a ship gives you freedom to walk to the edge of the deck and look more closely at the water. The guardrail on a beautiful mountain overlook gives you the freedom to go the very edge and view

God's scenic wonders with the confident assurance that you won't slip and fall. A fence around a playground assures the small child he can run and play freely without having to worry about the danger of unthinkingly darting into the street. (Tests *prove* that when the fence is removed the kids concentrate activities in the center of the playground and use far less of the area.)

I shall never forget an incident which took place about three months after I committed my life to the Lord. A young girl had been abducted, and there was much concern for her life. Thousands of people uttered tens of thousands of prayers, but I shall never forget one of them. Richard Peacock, our minister to adults, asked God to build a "ring of fire" around the girl. As he uttered those words, a chill swept over me and I *knew* she was safe in God's guardrail. To be in the arms of Jesus is to free you, and not bind you. Freedom from wrong, doubt, and fear enables you to go further and faster and to do more when you get there. I confess that this has been and is totally true in my own life.

THANK YOU, LORD, FOR MY FOOT

When yard-cutting time rolled around last April I pushed the lawn mower out and prepared to "get at it." I checked to see that we had gasoline in the tank (that's *all* I know how to do!) and started to crank it up. I pulled the cord a few times with zero results, so I backed off and caught my breath before I really got after it with a vengeance. I pulled the cord furiously time after time after time. *Then* I looked down and knew why the lawn mower hadn't started. My foot was under the housing, and I had on canvas shoes. I breathed a deeply felt prayer of thanksgiving and as I pulled the cord again—with my foot safely out of the way—I *knew* the lawn mower would start up this time. And it did.

Again, I'm sure the skeptics and critics would say it was "just a coincidence," but I say, "Thank You, Lord, for my foot." To me it makes sense that if He would die to save my soul He would keep a lawn mower from starting in order to save my foot. Of course, I also believe that God is listening each day when I ask Him to build a protective wall around me and mine. I know He was listening that day.

THE RIGHT PERSON

On Saturday before Christmas of 1975 I was scheduled to fly to Cleveland, Ohio, for a speaking engagement. I had come in from Portland, Oregon, the day before after a series of scheduling mishaps, boo-boos, and bad weather that would have had me climbing the walls before I turned my life over to the Lord. Since anything can happen to the airlines during the Christmas rush—and generally does—to be on the safe side I called on Friday night to verify my flight. They gave me the bad news: I had been cancelled when I missed a connection in Seattle. Obviously, somebody had goofed. It could have been me, it could have been the airlines, or it could have been both of us. That's not important. The only thing that concerned me was I had no seat on the plane to Cleveland to fill an engagement I had scheduled over six months earlier.

So, what do you do when the planes are so full that they have stopped booking stand-by reservations and when even the preferred stand-by list on the only really logical flight for me to catch had twenty-six people on it? I told my story to the ticket agent and was very careful not to take my frustration out on her since she had nothing to do with creating the problem. She listened sympathetically and turned me over to her supervisor, a super-nice girl who introduced a glimmer of hope.

JUST ONE SEAT

She suggested I go to the airport three hours early the next day and get in line. On the way to the airport, as I had been doing during the night, I prayed if it were the Lord's will, He would get me on that plane. I knew anything was possible, so I specifically prayed God would lead me to the person who could get me on that plane. (Since I was praying, I went ahead and asked for a good seat on the best flight.) When I stepped in line there were at least thirty people in front of me, and in nothing flat a dozen more got in line behind me. I prepared for a long wait. Then, by the strangest coincidence, one of the floor people, whom I did not know, came directly to me—and *only* to me—and told me if I walked down to the next terminal (about 100 yards away), the lines wouldn't be nearly so long.

I thanked him and the Lord and started my walk. Sure enough, there were only about three people in line, and in short order I was in front of the ticket agent telling my story. I told it exactly as it happened, without blaming anyone but stressing the urgency of my situation. The agent was pleasant and sympathetic, but as he kept pressing those computer buttons and checking the alternatives he kept shaking his head, in the wrong direction. After about ten minutes he told me there was no way I could get to Cleveland that day. At this point my memory is a little foggy as to exactly what happened. A supervisor, by coincidence, was standing close by. I don't remember whether he voluntarily offered to help or whether the ticket agent asked him to help. At any rate, he entered the picture and started pressing those computer buttons. I never saw a guy so persistent. He must have pressed every button at least a dozen times. Finally, he looked at the agent, smiled, and said, "I didn't see a thing but one seat for Mr. Ziglar to be on his way to Cleveland."

I'm certain that many people would say, "big deal"—with more than a trace of sarcasm. But to *anyone* who has ever flown out of the Dallas-Fort Worth Airport on the Saturday before Christmas to *any* major city without a guaranteed seat at least thirty days in advance, it is more than just a "big deal." It's a major miracle! Fortunately, the God I worship specializes in miracles for His people—and you can rest assured, it's *not* a coincidence.

MAY I JOIN YOU?

In the summer of 1976 I spoke to a large group of sales people in Baton Rouge, Louisiana. The next morning I arose fairly early and went down for breakfast, expecting to eat a leisurely solitary breakfast. However, as I entered the dining room I saw a group of about twenty men having breakfast, so I asked if I could join them. They instantly and enthusiastically urged me to be their guest. The non-Christian will undoubtedly feel I was presumptuous and forward to intrude on a meeting of "strangers." The Christian instantly knows those men were not strangers. They were "brothers," and I immediately recognized them as such because, by coincidence, they were all carrying the same book, the one God wrote, the Holy Bible. The next thirty minutes were exciting. The men came from every walk of life— three of them had played on the National Champion LSU football team of 1958, two of them had been members of the famed "Chinese Bandits" defensive team—*all* of them were brothers.

To me one of the most exciting benefits of knowing Jesus Christ is having a "family" in every city I have ever visited. Whether I'm speaking in Brisbane, Australia, or Friona, Texas, I *know* that when I honor my Lord I will instantly have the prayer support of my brothers and sisters in the audience. I also know when the session is over some members of that audience will come forth and express their Christian love. I've got to confess this one thing gives me as much joy as just about anything that happens in my life. It's a real *now* benefit.

As I wrote those last words on this flight from Louisville, Kentucky, to Chicago, Illinois, I glanced across the aisle in time to see a beautiful young girl bow in prayer before she started to eat. My heart jumped with joy as I stepped over to greet her. The skeptic would say, "just a coincidence" that you should be writing about having Christian brothers and sisters all over the world and then meet Coretta Bather from Louisville on the plane. I believe the Lord was reminding me I have "family" not only all over the world but *above* the world, as well. Praise God!

IF A COINCIDENCE—WHY NOT BEFORE?

As the months and years go by and I really dig into the Bible more and more, every bit of knowledge increases my conviction and love. As I grow in love for my fellow man and for the Lord, too many things happen that cannot be put down as coincidences. Sales come my way that have to be pure gifts. Don't misunderstand. I'm working harder and more enthusiastically than ever before. Nonbelievers would simply say those sales are a result of positive thinking and positive working. Maybe so, but for many years I have been a positive thinker and a positive worker. Nevertheless, "I never had it so good!" or had so much fun in the process. The question is, "If they are just coincidences, why have there been more of them for my benefit in the last seven years than in the previous forty-five years?"

POSITIVE THINKING VERSUS POSITIVE BELIEVING

As I have indicated, I have always been a positive thinker; but I would like to explain the enormous difference between positive thinking and positive believing. Positive thinking is the optimistic hope, not necessarily based on any facts, that you can accomplish the near-impossible. I have seen some incredible things happen as a direct result of positive thinking. Positive believing is the same optimistic hope that you're going to be able to accomplish some incredible things, but it is undergirded with solid evidence that your positive thinking is fully justified. By analogy, let me give you an example, albeit a slightly ridiculous one. If I were to say that I thought I could whip Muhammed Ali, that would be positive thinking. If I *attempted* to whip Ali, it would be idiotic thinking. I'm too old, too slow, and too scared. Not only that, but I have a low threshold for pain and don't really want to whip him or anyone else. However, if I *really* thought I could, then I could do a better job than if I *knew* I couldn't. But, again, I say the results would be disaster for me. Positive believing, however, would be in evidence if Larry Holmes were to say, "I believe I can whip Muhammed Ali." The reasons are many. First, he has won thirty-two consecutive fights and at this writing is the heavyweight champion of the world. Second, Holmes is younger and his star is rising; Ali, by his own admission, is over the hill. Third, Holmes trains twelve months out of the year, while Ali trains only for the fights scheduled. In a nutshell, positive thinking is optimistic hope, while positive believing is the same optimistic hope built on a solid foundation of substantial evidence that you can accomplish what you believe you can.

As a non-Christian, I had a considerable amount of optimistic hope. With this "positive thinking," I did some good things and reached some of my objectives in life. By the same token, I occasionally got into trouble because my optimism had no real foundation. When I turned my life over to Jesus Christ, I retained all of the same positive thinking and optimistic hope I had previously possessed. However, when I added the deep conviction and belief that comes from trusting Jesus Christ as Lord and Savior, I had a solid foundation upon which to base my optimistic hope. After all, when the Creator of the universe gives you scriptural references assuring you that if you believe, you can, who am I to doubt the Scriptures? When He says, "Ye have not because ye ask not," then I can correct my lack by simply asking for it. When He says, "What I have done ye can do also, and even greater works than these," then I correct my negativism by believing what our Lord says. In short, with the continuous reassurance that all things are possible to him who believes, my positive thinking changed to positive believing. This accounts for the substantial increase in effectiveness in my personal, family, and business life.

A SPECIAL ENTREE FOR CONCERNED PARENTS
SPANK THEM AND TAKE THEM TO CHURCH

All responsible parents want the best for their children. One of the *worst* things that can happen to our children is an involvement with drugs. Dr. Forest Tennant at UCLA found, after a comprehensive study of the drug problem among the G.I.'s in Germany, only two deterrents among the men as far as drug usage was concerned: those who had been regularly and moderately spanked and had attended church fifty or more times *before* they were fifteen years old had a much lower incidence of drug usage. Since Christian parents have a much better chance of keeping their children off drugs, this is quite a *now* advantage— and another good reason for serving Jesus now.

REMEMBER: The more you thank God for what you have, the more you will have to thank God for.

First "Thank You" Date _____

Second "Thank You" Date _____

THANK YOU, LORD

FOR:

1. _____

2. _____

3. _____

4. _____

5. _____

6. _____

7. _____

8. _____

9. _____

10. _____

11. _____

12. _____

Don't count the things you do.
Do the things which count.

CHAPTER TWELVE

I Can't Understand

Since these are the *Confessions of A Happy Christian,* I guess I should confess that since I have turned my life over to the Lord I can't understand why you don't do the same thing. I'll be the first to admit that for years I lived in that gray or twilight zone of not really believing, and yet not really disbelieving. Now that I do believe and so completely enjoy the *now* benefits of serving Jesus, I can't understand why *everybody* doesn't immediately do the same thing!

However, I am all too familiar with the two enormous problems which confront you. First, you have been fed a tremendous amount of negative garbage for a long time as a member of today's cynical society. This includes a lot of well-intentioned but sadly misguided propaganda from members of the cultist groups, as well as some ordained ministers from legitimate churches who harp on all the things *you* have to do to be saved. Combine this with the natural negativisms that permeate our society (even the weatherman tells us we have a 40 percent chance of rain, instead of saying we have a 60 percent chance of sunshine!) and throw in the fact that Satan himself keeps spreading all the propaganda about what you "give up" and "can't do" when you serve Christ. With these factors there is little wonder why so many people close their minds and hearts, throw up their hands in despair, and declare that Christ demands the impossible. The tragedy is that the individual is so close to God's Kingdom the moment he throws up his hands and acknowledges he "can't do it." I repeat for emphasis that *no human being* can do it. Oh, that some loving, scripturally sound Christian were

189

close to that individual who reaches that point of despair, because the Scripture is so clear that *you* can't—but you *and* God can.

YOU ARE NOT GOOD ENOUGH

Over the years there were many occasions when I contemplated straightening up, cleaning up, and getting back into my church life. I felt I would not be acceptable to the Lord in my present condition, and that *I* had to do something about myself before *I* would be worthy to serve. Not long after I turned my life over to the Lord, my family left to go to Mississippi for a few days to visit our families. The decision to make the visit was a sudden one, and my redhead did not have time to do the laundry. I assured her I would take care of it. My "taking care of it" meant taking it to the laundry because I just don't like to fool with a washing machine. (Since I've never washed a load of clothes, I might not even know how.) I threw the clothes in the trunk with the full expectation of stopping by the cleaners that day. Then I forgot all about those dirty clothes for about three days. When I did remember them they were a disaster. The spare tire in the trunk had worked loose and ended up on top of the clothes, forcing them against a greasy jack and ultimately causing them to come undone. Dirt, grease, and tire-black can truly wreak havoc on clothes.

When I got them together I was so embarrassed about their appearance I literally backed into the laundry and up to the counter. The lady in charge was somewhat amazed—and amused—at my conduct, so she asked me what I was doing. I sheepishly explained that the clothes were such a mess that I was embarrassed to bring them in. She laughingly assured me it was all right and they would be glad to take care of them. I persisted by explaining I could have at least dusted them off and straightened them up a bit. Then she said something which had a dramatic impact on my life. "Mr. Ziglar," she said, "the only reason we are here is to clean up your dirty clothes, so we're glad they are a mess. We're even glad you can't clean them up because if you and all other people could clean up their laundry, there would be no reason for our being here." Then it hit me like a ton of bricks: if we could "clean up" the mess we have made of our lives there would have been no need for Calvary, no need for a Savior.

I say to you with a prayer in my heart that you can't "clean up" your life. If you're waiting to stop drinking, smoking, swearing, lying, and cheating so you will be worthy of knowing the Lord *before* you turn your life over to Him, you will *never* know Jesus personally. If you are waiting until you seek forgiveness from one you have wronged or to end an adulterous affair *before* you come to the throne of grace, you will *never* know Jesus. You, in your strength and will, just can't clean up your life, but if you will come just as you are, He will take you, love you, save you, forgive you, and invite you to live with Him forever. That's what He did for me, and I praise Him and thank Him many times every day for it.

This should have been obvious from the beginning, but the old saying that "it takes only a second to send a message twenty-five thousand miles around the world, but often takes years for it to penetrate the last quarter inch of bone," is really appropriate here. The purpose of the laundry is to clean dirty clothes. The purpose of Jesus Christ and *the* reason He came to earth is to do something for you, me, and all of mankind that we *cannot* do for ourselves. He came to "clean up" our lives, to wash away our sins, so that one day we will stand in front of the judgment seat of Christ spotless. Regardless of how "dirty" you are, He will wash you as white as snow. If you're waiting to clean yourself up before you get back into the mainstream of Christian commitment and serving the Lord, my friend, you're going to have a forever wait.

IT'S TIME TO START

One of the most difficult things for this author to do is to stop writing and bid you goodbye in print. It was especially difficult this time because so much more is at stake than ever before. The two major objectives of this book, in addition to selling the positive benefits of serving Christ now, are to persuade you to open your heart to Christ if you don't already know Him and to share Christ with others if you do know Him.

I was much in thought and prayer as to how to conclude this book in a manner that would expose any emptiness in your heart and encourage you to finish it on your knees as you invite Christ to completely take over your life. The way to end the book came to me fittingly enough in church on the first day of 1978. It's proper, and I believe providential, that the conclusion came at the beginning of the year, because it could be symbolic for you. Maybe, just maybe, the example God gave me through our pastor is God's way of saying to you that the final words in this book will be the beginning of a whole new world for you.

A MOTHER'S LOVE

Businessman Don Carter and his family were flying in to Dallas from Montana in their MU-2 plane when disaster struck. Visibility was poor and Don, a cautious, experienced pilot, struck a probe light (the blinking red lights that guide pilots into airfields) and crashlanded short of the runway. Injuries to the family were relatively minor, with the exception of son Ronnie who was badly cut on his head but has recuperated beautifully. However, Don, himself, was painfully and severely injured. All of the bones around his left eye and his upper jaw were broken and severely smashed. Surgery was extensive and Don's condition was critical. It is at this point that Dr. Criswell entered the picture and told the story.

NO VISITORS, PLEASE

The morning after the night of surgery the doctors were so concerned about Don's condition that they were taking hundreds of X-rays and tests. Dr. Criswell had been waiting at the hospital with Mary Crowley, Don's mother, for four hours. Because of the seriousness of his condition, the doctors had performed a tracheotomy on Don before surgery. Finally, when he was taken to the intensive care unit, Mary Crowley and Dr. Criswell were allowed to enter the room. With Mary on one side of the bed and Dr. Criswell on the other, they looked down on a face which was so badly swollen it was barely recognizable. Mary took Don's hand and softly, tenderly kissed it, gently and with the love known only to a deeply devoted mother. Dr. Criswell, to use his own words, prayed as best he knew from his fifty years of experience as a pastor and his nearly sixty years of walking with and loving the Lord. Then Mary Crowley prayed for her son. The prayer was too holy for Dr. Criswell to feel at liberty to share with the congregation of which I was privileged to be a part. It was a mother's prayer for her son, but it was more. It was the prayer of a dedicated Christian who long ago committed her life, her family, and her business to Jesus Christ. From the depths of her love and her faith, born and nurtured through a long and faithful walk with Jesus Christ, she asked for and received assurance that Don's life would be spared.

So beautiful and moving was the prayer, so total was this mother's love for her son, so obvious was her knowledge of His will and His love for her son, so deep was this special child of God's faith in her Lord and Savior, so total was her trust as she poured out her heart to Him, that, in Dr. Criswell's words, "I felt so pale in comparison, so much like a paid preacher, so inadequate and insincere in the prayer I had prayed."

Those of us who know and love Dr. Criswell feel these words are far too harsh and cruel for anyone to think about using to describe such a godly man who has led so many countless thousands to the Throne of Grace. Yet, we surely know what our pastor is saying. Not that his prayers were insincere, or unheeded, because the Bible clearly says that "The fervent prayer of a righteous man availeth much." It's just that Mary Crowley's love for her son, who is also God's son, and her love for Jesus Christ was the love that only a mother can know, so her prayer was the prayer that only a Christian mother could know and feel deeply enough to pray. With a mother praying *for* the son she loves *to* the God she loves, you've just got to know that since the God she was praying to loves mother and son, even more than the love they have for each other, that He was deeply concerned about *both* of His children. He heard the prayers, and even as I write these words on the first day of this new year, Don Carter is well on his way to a miraculous recovery. Thank You, Lord. Needless to say, the prayers of the countless thousands of Don's friends and associates also played a significant part in his recovery.

I'm personally convinced the prayer and love deposits which Mary Crowley had been making for so many years were all made available to her—with interest—at that moment of great need. It's not that our Lord would listen any less to a new believer. But love is a special language, and since God is love, He heard the prayers of a mother who for so long had spoken the language so well. As Dr. Criswell, who was deeply involved emotionally, was telling the story, the realization of the power of love expressed through prayer hit me again. I was reminded of how tremendously blessed I have been to have had a mother who daily, in deep love, lifted my name in prayer. How grateful I am for a wife who has prayed so much and so hard for me. How lucky to have children who know the Lord and who pray for me regularly. In time of deep need, I'm convinced, the prayers of one who deeply loves the one whose name is lifted in prayer is prayer at its highest, holiest, most effective best.

MY FINAL CONFESSION

It is my fervent prayer you have seen Jesus in the pages of this book and are now ready to accept Him as Savior and make Him Lord of your life. If you already know Him as Lord and Savior, it is my prayer you will make the total commitment to serve Him in everything you do so you will enjoy more of what God has to offer in this world.

If you do not know Jesus but are now ready to acknowledge Him as Lord and Savior, then wherever you are and whatever you are doing, just quietly close your eyes and if possible get down on your knees and repeat this little prayer: "Lord, I know You are God's only begotten Son, that You were born of the Virgin Mary, and You lived a perfect life on earth; that You died on the cross and went to the grave, where You stayed three days before You arose triumphant over death. I know, Lord, Your blood was shed to wash away my sins, and I ask You now to forgive my sins and accept me into Your Kingdom of eternal life. Thank You, Lord. It's in the Name of Jesus that I pray, and for His sake. Amen."

GET BUSY AND SERVE THE LORD

Now, my new Brother or Sister in Christ, I urge you to immediately seek the company of other believers. You can best do this through your local churches. The only word of caution I offer is that you make absolutely certain the church you select is preaching *all* of the Bible and *only* the Bible as God's Holy Word. If the minister, pastor, or priest does not believe that the entire Bible—*all* of it—is the inspired Word of God, I urge you to seek another church. I especially urge you to move to another church if any other book is introduced as the divinely inspired word of God. I also urge you to get a good reference Bible and set aside some time *every* day to study God's Word. There are many organizations and study aids available which are tremendously helpful.

Your new life as a Christian can be exciting and rewarding in a thousand ways, but surely the most exciting and rewarding one occurs when you have the privilege of introducing someone else to the Lord. I urge you to prayerfully take advantage of that opportunity as often as possible. Throughout this book you will find some information which I believe will add effectiveness to your witness. Share the *now* benefits, the joy, peace, and power which you personally experience as you serve Christ.

I'm going to assume that as you finish this book you have made—either earlier or at this time—a firm commitment to trust Jesus Christ with your soul. Therefore I close by concluding that if you have accepted Christ as Lord, then I know you will have a good forever—which means I'll SEE YOU AT THE TOP.

REMEMBER: The more you thank God for what you have, the more you will have to thank God for.

First "Thank You" Date _____

Second "Thank You" Date _____

THANK YOU, LORD

FOR:

1. _____

2. _____

3. _____

4. _____

5. _____

6. _____

7. _____

8. _____

9. _____

10. _____

11. _____

12. _____

My favorite definition of a Christian:
a person who leads someone to Jesus Christ.

Thank You Daddy

Those were the words with which my eldest daughter greeted me when I returned to the landing on the mezzanine at the hotel. We were there for a meeting and I had just finished speaking. My son-in-law, Chad Witmeyer, and my son, Tom, were taking our materials back to the car and Suzan was waiting for me. She hugged me and kissed me and said, "Thank you, Daddy, for finding Jesus seven years ago, because if you hadn't found Him then, I wouldn't know Him now." Then I did what my Christian brothers and sisters would expect me to do. I hugged and kissed her and cried a little. Then I hugged her and kissed her and shed a few more tears.

The story does go back to that date in July, 1972, when I committed my life to Christ and found such joy and peace and excitement that I wanted everyone in the world to share it with me. Naturally, I especially wanted those whom God had entrusted to my care to share it with me. One by one they had come into the fold and had known the joy of the Lord. But, Suzan, my oldest daughter, simply had not opened her heart to salvation. This final confession is one of those "NOW IT CAN BE TOLD" stories. To be candid with you, every word, every sentence, every phrase, every thought, every paragraph in the first printing of CONFESSIONS OF A HAPPY CHRISTIAN had been written specifically for Suzan.

When I finished the initial draft, for some reason I felt no compelling urge to complete the book. For over a year the manuscript lay largely untouched. Then, through events already mentioned, I felt the urge to complete it. As I shared my additional experiences on the rewrite, God continued to draw me closer to Him. He blessed me in incredible and ever-increasing ways, and the compulsion to complete the book for Suzan was overwhelming. It was my feeling that God would use it to claim her for His Kingdom.

Finally, the long-awaited day arrived and the book was in the hands of the publisher. After what seemed like an eternity, we had our own copies and I immediately gave each member of my family a copy. They all started reading, with the exception of Suzan and her husband, whom she had married since I originally started the book.

PATIENCE, DAD, PATIENCE

Undoubtedly the toughest assignment I have ever had was the self-imposed one of not asking them if they were reading CONFESSIONS. However, I very definitely felt that I must not push them to read it. Anxiously I waited as the days stretched into weeks. Then they got involved with a direct sales company through a Godly couple who have all the qualities you look for in successful people. They were successful spiritually, as a family, and as business people. They were loving and caring, and they had large numbers of associates who were cut from the same bolt of cloth. In this kind of an environment, Suzan and Chad were inspired to explore good literature, and soon they even started attending church. But they were still not reading CONFESSIONS OF A HAPPY CHRISTIAN. Then one night it happened. Suzan opened the book and started to read. She called me, and the excitement in her voice was unmistakable as she described her feelings while reading. She said she had never seen so much joy and happiness jump off the pages of any book. I breathed a prayer of thanksgiving and knew that the Lord's timing was working on His schedule, whether it was on mine or not.

After a couple of weeks and a few visits, Suzan and Chad were at our home one Sunday afternoon. I felt strongly that they were ready to commit their lives to Christ. After carefully and prayerfully leading them through what I believed were the necessary steps, I asked them if they were ready to accept Christ as Lord and commit their lives to him. Chad responded that he felt that he already had. This thrilled us tremendously not only because of our love and concern for Chad, but also because we were hopeful that his commitment and leadership would encourage Suzan. However, when I asked Suzan if she was ready to make her commitment, she responded in the negative. I was stunned, heartbroken, and deeply disappointed by her answer, but I had learned that when you leave things up to the Lord, they happen. Still, I must confess that I also knew that when the Holy Spirit beckons and you decline, that you might not get that call again, so I was distressed. The next four days I was much in prayer as I asked God to claim Suzan for His very own, so you can just imagine the feeling of total exhilaration I felt when Suzan gave me the good news.

With a light step and a grateful heart, I walked downstairs with Suzan to meet Chad and Tom in the restaurant for a snack. We were alone for a couple of moments before Tom and Chad came back in. When they sat down, I turned to Tom and said, "Son, guess who Suzan just met?" Temporarily there was a stunned expression on his face and then his little eyes started to fill and he bowed his head and wept. Those of you who have loved ones who have come to know the Lord after you met Him surely know the feeling of total joy and ecstasy that came into my heart when Suzan made her commitment to Christ.

I was tempted to label this my final confession, but unless God calls me home immediately, I do not believe it will be my final one. I continue to be astonished every day at His goodness, His love, His generosity, and His mercy, so I suspect I will have many final blessings to confess. Praise His Holy Name!

Epilogue

We shed tears of pure joy when Suzan accepted Christ as her Savior, and then, on May 13, 1995, our Suzan closed her eyes for the last time and went home to be with the Lord. Our tears were many; our hearts were broken. But at the same time, we felt unspeakable joy because we knew our Suzan would never be ill again. She would bask in the glory of the Lord she came to love so much. Even today we still weep on occasion, but our total assurance that she is safe with Christ more than covers our tears, and as time goes on, our thoughts are more and more of her in the perfect health she now enjoys and the incredibly beautiful memories we have of the joy she brought to us during her forty-six years of life with us. We are eternally grateful that God trusted us with her life, and let us enjoy and love her all those years.

After Suzan's death I immediately started journaling and it was comforting and very helpful in dealing with my grief. Out of the journaling came *Confessions of a Grieving Christian*, and an even deeper commitment to my Lord, my family, and what God has called me to do. Tragically, something like 80 percent of couples divorce after the death of a child, but my wife and I grew infinitely closer and often observe that we do not know how we could have handled the death of our daughter had we not known Christ, but that through Him, His promises and assurances, we drew infinitely closer than ever before. Here's hoping this book will be a blessing to you and that you will find eternal peace through knowing Christ as your Lord and Savior.

ALSO BY ZIG ZIGLAR

Zig Ziglar's inspirational best seller *See You at the Top*, the ninth biggest-selling religious book in America in 1977, is available in bookstores everywhere. More than 1,400,000 hardcover copies have been sold, and editions have also been published in French and Spanish. The "I Can" course based on the book is taught in many schools.

See You at the Top identifies the qualities necessary for a richer life and teaches how to develop those qualities. It offers fifteen specific steps to build a better self-image. More than eight hundred examples, illustrations, analogies, and one-liners hold the reader's interest while providing solid, commonsense procedures for getting more out of this life—without jeopardizing the next one.

Zig Ziglar's books are available from the publisher:

Pelican Publishing Company
1000 Burmaster Street
Gretna, Louisiana 70053

Information concerning Zig Ziglar's cassette recordings, four-day Richer Life seminars, and the "I Can" course for schools may be obtained from:

Zig Ziglar Training Systems
15303 Dallas Pkwy., Ste. 550
Addison, TX 75001
(972) 233-9191

WHAT DOES IT MEAN?

The fish was the sign used by early Roman Christians. During those days of persecution, when two Christians met, and neither knew with certainty the other was a Christian, one would take his stave and draw a line ⌒ in the dust. The second would then draw a second line ⊂⋉ . Many Christians today have pins or decals with this sign to let others know they are Christians.

When I committed my life to serving Him, I sought a way to witness. As a professional salesman I knew that if a method of witnessing could be devised so that people inquired or initiated the conversation, it would provide me with an excellent witnessing opportunity. The idea of the numeral *seven* seemed especially appropriate, since it symbolizes God's number of completion. It also is the perfect number. Virtually every day of my life someone asks the question, "What does the seven on the fish mean?" This gives me that priceless privilege of sharing Jesus Christ with others.

A special pamphlet explaining the ⌒⋉ and a special pin like the one described (14-carat gold-plated) are now available. If you would like one of the pins and pamphlets, please send a check or money order for $2 to:

Zig Ziglar Training Systems
15303 Dallas Pkwy., Ste. 550
Addison, TX 75001   (972) 233-9191

Note: All profits from the sale of the pin go to spreading the Good News about Jesus Christ.